Father of The Stranger

Keith,

Thanks you for your
service! I hope you
enjoy reading my
story!

Gent

Father of The Stranger

A Story of the Second

Military Police Unit at Abu Ghraib

Gerit Wasserman

Published by Battle Cross Publications

ISBN: 978-0-692-43693-6

Printed in the United States of America

Cover Photo: Aaron Osborne

To Lt. Tania Sharpe . . .
Thanks for Everything!

Contents

Introduction

ON THE FACE OF IT, my getting the honor of writing an introduction to this remarkable memoir seems as inappropriate as it is unlikely. Yet, here we are. The author of this story will not tell you that he's a hero because he thinks he is not. I think he is and I'll say again, it is a great and singular honor to get to say a few words here at the start of this important book.

Gerit Wasserman reached out to me from his life on the eastern seaboard, three-thousand miles away from where I was living at my winter home in Tucson. We'd never spoken, never met. I was/am best known as an author of novels marketed to teens and young adults. Sarge, as I soon came to call him, queried whether or not I'd be willing to take a look at his story and perhaps, as he phrased, "help get it that last few yards across the goal line." My first reaction, although I didn't say it to him, was, why would I? Why should I? I don't now, and have never had a red, white and blue magnetic ribbon attached to the back of my car; I don't even fly the flag out in front of my house so that all my neighbors know how patriotic I am. But these very facts, my absence of a demonstrable patriotism, answered my questions for me.

Truth is, I never served. In fact, I cut my political teeth and consciousness during the Vietnam Era, by opposing that war. But I was gung-ho about Iraq in the aftermath of 9/11. I supported the war, despite some reservations. And then I came to believe I was wrong. Abu Ghraib crystalized all my doubts, the horrifying pictures of prisoner abuse sickened me. What on earth were we doing in that part of the world intervening in a conflict between

1

warring factions as old and violent as the one that raged between Catholics and Protestants for hundreds of years?

So the odds were low that I'd be interested in helping this guy I'd never met tell his war memoir of his service in Iraq, especially when I found out that he had served as a Military Policeman at. . . Abu Ghraib!

Probably it was the very inappropriateness and weirdness of his query that made me decide to give his story a quick perusal. He sent me the manuscript in an email attachment and I told him that I'd take a look. Truthfully, I doubted that there would be much of anything I could or would want to do. But as soon as I started to read, political considerations disappeared. This isn't a story about politics; it is a story about, among other things, what war does to men and what it takes to hold onto the best of ones self and resist the darker callings.

That was several hundred emails ago, and after several hundred hours of time spent trying to help him improve the fundamentals of writing/language/etc. of the story he wanted to tell. Sarge was and is NOT a writer, but he indeed had a hell of a story. And it soon became, to me, my duty to help him get it as good as he/we could.

During this process Sarge and I became friends. And I was able to double-down on this by becoming acquainted with his best buddies from his service in Iraq. This is an honor I am proud of and one I take seriously.

As you read this story and get to know these soldiers, your patriotism will increase, your pride in our country will swell because these men went into the breach, as the first wave of MP's to serve at Abu Ghraib in the immediate aftermath of the revelations of alleged abuses occurring there. They had nothing to do with the mess, other than to try and survive the consequences of it and do their best to clean it up.

Sgt. Wasserman's memoir centers on a particular event, while giving a background of he and his comrades' time spent in harm's way. The story rings true because it is true. It is told without artifice or 'writer's tricks,' direct, believable, and powerful.

We are caught-up in a society polarized by opposing political viewpoints. But *Father of The Stranger* reminds us of what it means to be an American and a citizen soldier. Again, and finally, I am honored to have been able to perhaps help in some small way Sgt. Wasserman tell his story of his time at Abu Ghraib. It is a story worth reading and more than worth remembering.

Terry Trueman
Printz Honor Author of *Stuck In Neutral*

Preface

I DECIDED TO WRITE THIS book at the suggestion of my sister, Terri, as a way to preserve details of my experience of the war in Iraq before they begin fade over time. We were average citizen-soldiers who were called up and deployed, and we saw our service as a privilege rather than a burden. When it was over, we went back to our families, jobs and communities believing we had given nothing less than our best.

I have chosen to tell this story as it is represented by a one-week slice, towards the end of our deployment. It could, however, have literally been any three soldiers or other groups of missions or events on another day, and the story told would not change all that much. Every MP's job was interchangeable with another, and every soldier was working as hard as the next.

This book was not necessarily written for a military audience. Soldiers who have gone to Iraq or Afghanistan have their own experiences, and I believe that most of our fighting men and women already know how strange events can unfold on the battlefield.

Father of the Stranger was written for the average person. It was also written for the worried parents and grandparents who are sending their loved ones off to a war that barely makes a ripple in our everyday pond in the United States. I want people to know that their neighbors and co-workers are the soldiers who went off to fight a war to defend this country. These men and women hoped above all hope to make a difference somehow, and they believed it was better to fight our enemies on a foreign battlefield rather than here at home. We believed that we were part of something bigger than any one of us is alone and greater than all of us together. Defending our nation against all enemies was the noblest of causes.

The events I describe are based primarily on my own memories. Some parts of the stories have been compacted, and in some cases, the events are an amalgamation of the collective memories of the men that served with me. I have changed the names of many of the individuals mentioned in this book to protect their identities as much as possible and have reconstructed various conversations to the best of my ability and as accurately as possible to ensure the integrity of the story. I did not exaggerate the events, but used as much imagery as necessary to paint an accurate picture of the experience. If inaccuracies occur, they are my responsibility and mine alone.

I did not attempt to address the scandal that would eventually unfold under our feet or determine the guilt or innocence of any party involved in those events. We had a daunting task continuing the mission in the face of blistering attacks on the prison and with the media reporting the scandal. Readers looking for dark secrets or untold scandals won't find them in this book. I went to some lengths not to discuss tactics or training used by military police units, and I did not reveal any information that cannot be found through public sources. I used Abu Ghraib as a backdrop the same way a photographer uses a black curtain to highlight the subjects he is trying to capture. At the same time, I tried to give the reader a true picture of daily life at the prison.

This story does not and cannot know the feelings, emotions and experiences of other soldiers in other parts of Iraq. I am sure that a Marine fighting house-to-house in Fallujah had a much different experience than we had at Abu Ghraib. We have never considered ourselves heroes or cowards, just average soldiers trying to do a good job under strenuous circumstances. I want people to know that teamwork counts, friends matter, and, regardless of what you do or how well you perform, something will happen that you cannot control. Insurance companies call this an "Act of God." In our case, I believe the Act of God could have been the "insurance company" that gave us one unusual, final mission.

Triple strands of razor wire surrounded the perimeter, and soldiers who paced the perimeter watched us curiously. I am sure they knew we were their relief. I told myself,

I know they're glad we're here.

Always a Soldier

WHEN I WAS GROWING UP in southeastern Virginia, I lived in a somewhat small and isolated neighborhood. The other boys in the neighborhood and I would often play army in a partially overgrown field behind my house. We built forts, climbed trees, and threw dirt clods like hand grenades. We watched war movies on TV and collected comic books in which the hero always won. Even then, in the back of my mind, I always believed that military service would eventually enter into my life. But as I became a teenager, my thoughts drifted to girls, cars, sports, and maybe a part-time job to support those three interests.

After graduating from high school, I had no solid college or career plan. The friends I grew up with slowly started to peel off and go in their separate directions. One evening, my best friend and I were leaning against his car bouncing a tennis ball and talking about what to do next. He mentioned that he had talked with a National Guard recruiter and asked if I was interested in joining with him on the buddy system. I had been out of high school for six or eight months, and my job prospects were just laborer positions. I thought I was in love, but my girlfriend's mother hated me, and I had junk for a car. A few weeks later, my buddy and I were on a plane to Fort Bliss, Texas, for basic training and advanced individual training or AIT as an Air Defense Artillery Crewman. We had joined the Virginia Army National Guard.

Twenty or so years later, I found myself to be average. College was off and on, based mostly on my finances. I was a good part-time soldier and had gone through some good army training schools, but my military career had its highs and lows. At one point in my career I had attended a general instructor-training course, and, for more than a year afterwards, I was assigned with the air defense school out of Fort Bliss, Texas, teaching the Stinger Missile System to transitioning National Guard units. When the Army National Guard eventually realigned our battalion, I found myself out of a job and switched over to the Army Reserves. There, I picked up another military occupational skill (MOS) as well as gained some valuable secondary skills, one of which was a Combat Lifesaver course. Nevertheless, I had also missed opportunities for advancement. As a member of the Reserves or National Guard, I found that the training and schools necessary for promotion could sometimes be hard to work into a civilian career, which usually resulted in my staying in the same military position for longer periods than if I had been on active duty. My civilian career in the architectural & engineering field also had its challenges. I had started as an entry-level draftsman and was trying to work my way up to an elusive top. Some employers did not always understand or agree with the fact that I was not available some weekends and that my annual training period was not my vacation. Additionally, I could be called into active duty for extended periods, during which they had to keep my civilian job available. This usually resulted in a lack of upward mobility. Taking on school part-time, having a family, and multi-tasking life's day-to-day activities, I found myself performing a well-orchestrated juggling act.

Still, I enjoyed the Army Reserve and valued my service to my country. By late 2003, everything in my life seemed balanced as a whole. I had married, and my wife and I were still in our honeymoon phase, enjoying the concept of being a couple. In June of that year, I had taken a job as a construction project manager, and that was giving me a new level of experience that I found rewarding. My son Kyle, from a previous relationship, was still relatively young and was a great kid. We had a good father-son relationship and watching him grow up was enjoyable. I had recently transitioned into a new reserve unit and had been accepted into the drill sergeants' academy, scheduled for January of 2004. I had come to admire the sergeants who wore the brown campaign hats and had tormented me during basic training, and I believed their mission was a mission I could fulfill.

On December 19, 2003, all of that balance shifted when I received a phone call at work from my reserve unit notifying me that I was slated for deployment. It did not have the same shock effect on me as it would eventually have on my wife, but I was surprised. At that time, our nation had already been at war for a little over two years and everyone in the military knew that deployment was a possibility at some point. However, this was two days before my wife's birthday and six days before Christmas.

I informed my boss of the call and left work immediately to tell my wife the news in person. She worked at a bank at the time. I sat in a small conference room while a receptionist went to find Nadaleane to tell her I was waiting. Since it was unusual for me to show up at her workplace, the first thing she asked was, "What's wrong?" When I told her I was scheduled for deployment overseas, to Iraq, her lip quivered and her eyes filled up with tears; she was devastated. I was more prepared for it and, in many ways, had hoped for it. On the other hand, Nadaleane had prayed the opposite. I had been deployed overseas before, but nothing of this magnitude. In any case, I felt that if I wore the uniform I had an obligation to do what my country asked when called. This was my opportunity to make that contribution.

I had changed my MOS or specialty when I enlisted in the Army Reserve from Air Defense and Infantry to what was known as a 31B, Military Police. In the back of my mind, I had known this day was going to come sooner or later, although I hadn't told my wife and family. Military Police were always in high demand and usually were asked to carry out a variety of missions on military posts and in forward battle areas. These missions included convoy and route security, prison operations, personal escort duties, and perimeter defense, in addition to the vast array of general law enforcement duties. We were the all-purpose, fill-in soldiers when everyone else was either married to their bulky equipment or had limited mission capabilities. We often said to ourselves that MP actually stood for "multi-purpose."

In the wake of the 9/11 attacks, our nation had plunged itself into two wars. Reserve and National Guard units had been activated and sent overseas more often since the mid-1990s, but at that point, when it became apparent that we were in a prolonged shooting war, the operational tempo increased dramatically. At the time, nearly 40% of all units overseas in Iraq or Afghanistan were Reserve or National Guard and it did not appear that the percentage was going to decline anytime soon.

The timeline to get to my newly assigned unit was short. On Christmas Eve 2003, I received my orders, via e-mail, placing me on active duty and assigning me to my unit, an MP Battalion in Ohio. On New Year's Eve, I received my orders, again via e-mail, that deployed me to Iraq with that unit, still mobilizing. I had about ten days to pull my life together enough to leave it behind, pack up everything that the army had issued me and get myself to Fort Dix, New Jersey.

My reserve unit had five soldiers identified for deployment. Three were heading to training bases in the continental United States, and two of us were going overseas. This mobilization had caught my unit off guard as well. Many of the full-time reservists were taking leave during the holidays, and, for the most part, the unit was empty. I needed to get my wife signed up for medical insurance, get my hands on my records, arrange oversight for a rental property, tie up some loose ends at work, and say my goodbyes. Fortunately, I had gone through this process before, and my dad had always filled in the gaps for me when I was gone. Without a whole lot of discussion, I told him what I needed him to cover, handed him a notebook with most of the necessary paperwork, and told him we would figure the rest out on the run.

On January 6, 2004, one day after my son's seventh birthday, I left a very sad wife, a son, and my parents behind as I drove to Fort Dix. I arrived late in the afternoon with just a building number in hand to locate my company. I flagged down a Department of Defense police officer, who was able to help me locate the building. I walked in, found the operations officer that I had been communicating with, introduced myself, and was quickly integrated into 1st Squad, 1st Platoon, Headquarters Company of the 391st MP Battalion.

Over the course of our deployment, we would get to know each other well. Eventually, we built bonds that can only be understood by a group of people who go through the tempering process together and come out on the other side stronger than when they entered.

At the time, I don't think any us of actually knew specifically where we were going in Iraq or exactly how long we were going to be there. Our orders indicated eighteen months, but we knew things changed on a daily basis as the conditions changed. Our biggest concern was getting through the mobilization process, which included weapons qualifications, first-aid training, mission-specific training, lots of paperwork, medical evaluations and more shots than you can imagine. We wanted to be "boots on the ground" as quickly as possible. That was the catch phrase of the day.

Approximately two weeks into the mobilization, a rumor began to circulate that we were heading to a place called Abu Ghraib. At first, no one could even pronounce the name. We started to hear bits and pieces about some type of scandal, but rumor is what rumor is—nothing. However, they sped up our training tempo in an effort to get us out of Fort Dix a few days earlier than planned. None of us had any idea what was unfolding with the unit already on the ground at Abu Ghraib, or that an investigation was under way regarding what was to become the Army's black eye of the war.

After we arrived in Iraq and took over detainee operations, the totality of our circumstances began to set in and a formula to get everyone through this challenging mission was not readily available. The single, most important thing we knew was that we didn't want to end up like our predecessors. Regardless of the circumstances we were stuck with certain aspects of being MPs. Our job description required us to maintain around-the-clock operations all 365 days of the year. Also, in a detention environment when detainees were moved for any reason, it required MPs to escort them from place to place. The Forwarding Operation Base or FOB was big. It covered a few hundred acres and moving the detainees from one location to another within the FOB was one thing, but transporting them to other locations outside the wall was an effort and required coordination with other units, intelligence information and logistical support. The manpower had to be constantly adjusted to meet the changing dynamics, as the leadership responded to a fluid battlefield during a time of political uncertainty. However, the larger part of a MPs life, not just at Abu Ghraib, but anywhere, was getting through the daily grind. It was not glamorous or exciting by any stretch of the imagination and could allow a soldier to become complacent if not careful. Our daily grind was 90% boredom and monotony, 7% uncertainty, and 3% chaos. It was the last 3% that defined who we were and allowed us to establish a well-earned sense of pride in restoring America's honor.

Welcome to Your New Home

A CONVOY OF TRUCKS AND Humvee's drove through the opening in the high concrete perimeter wall and past the unusually shaped guard towers with deep overhangs. The engines whistled as the drivers shifted gears, pressed on the accelerator and pulled behind a group of buildings just inside another, inner set of walls. The driver shut the engine off, jumped down from the cab and walked to the rear of the truck to unhook the tailgate chain. The heavy door dropped with a metallic thud. One by one soldiers began to jump down and small clouds of dust mushroomed up as our feet hit the hard, but powdery ground.

Each of us looked around and saw buildings damaged from battle, vandalism and piles of debris scattered here and there. The walls had graffiti painted on them and a general lack of maintenance gave a glooming sense of abandonment. I thought to myself, *what a dump*. The driver stepped back as the rest of the soldiers unloaded and pulled duffle bags from the rear of the truck.

"Welcome to your new home. This is Abu Ghraib," he said.

Other men in other trucks were also unloading, and within a few minutes a company of soldiers were loosely assembled with duffle bags stacked in a small open area between two buildings. The driver jumped back into the cab and the engine whistled up again as black smoke shot from the exhaust stack. The trucks and Humvee's pulled away and parked in an area just outside where we were standing in a makeshift motor pool set up by the host unit.

Our captain gave the 1st Sergeant a tug on his sleeve and said, "Let's go find out where we're supposed to be and get a situation report."

"Roger that Sir," the 1st Sergeant replied and began walking towards a door marked TOC for Tactical Operations Center. It was the front office for the company commanders and the first sergeants, and pertinent information to the company went through the TOC.

We looked around and at each other, but this time the thought was translated into words, "What a stinking dump." Another soldier within ear shot repeated the sentiment, "What kind of a shit hole is this anyway?" I agreed. It looked as though we had landed in a junk yard on the moon. A morbid reminder was parked nearby, heavily damaged; a lone Humvee with most of the front end missing or mangled had been pulled aside awaiting disposal. We later learned that a Sergeant from the outgoing unit had died in a recent attack with an Improvised Explosive Device or IED on that vehicle.

The new war on terrorism had also given us a new term, the IED. It meant the same thing as the booby trap had meant in other wars, but the IED was more deadly and more vicious. They were typically assembled with old mortar rounds or artillery shells that had been modified with triggering devices to be set off on demand with cell phones. They were disguised in trash, road repairs, dead animals and any number of unsuspicious ways that allowed soldiers to pass them without notice until an insurgent was ready to detonate the device. The result was most often fatal.

Thinking back to less than two weeks before, we had left the frigid temperatures of New Jersey where we had mobilized and had traveled almost unceasingly for two days, through Germany and finally ending up in a large tent city in the Kuwaiti desert.

The tent cities were nothing more than places to hold soldiers until they became acclimated to the region and it allowed units assembling from different places to hold up until everyone could arrive. They had familiar names like Camp Virginia or Camp New York. Some catered to troops heading into the region, while others were specific to troops heading home and were a welcome relief for any soldier who had been in transit a while.

The camps themselves were not bad for the amount of time that you had to spend in them. They had large chow halls, an active morale, welfare and recreation program (MWR), telephones, computers and numerous other accommodations depending on what one was looking to do. As a whole they were not too shabby for something thrown up in the middle of a giant sandbox. It was hard to pinpoint their exact locations in reference to any specific city and the barren, seemingly featureless landscape gave us no clues to where we were other than in a desert. But based on the time it took us to get there from Al A Salem air base, Kuwait, we knew we had to be relatively close to the air base.

We waited out our time in the sandbox and then loaded onto C-130 cargo planes for the flight into what everyone knew as BIAP or Baghdad International Airport. The planes flew a corkscrew pattern into the airport to avoid potentially incoming ground fire or anti-aircraft missiles. The accommodations on the ground at BIAP were smaller and less luxurious than back in camp Virginia. Built entirely with sandbags, tents, and concrete, BIAP's purpose was to move troops in and out in about 24 hours. It was not comfortable enough to linger and dinner or breakfast was a box of MRE's available to whoever was hungry. We paid our penance at BIAP, and early the following morning, the outgoing unit that we were sent to relieve came to pick us up. They rolled in with about a half a dozen 2 ½ ton trucks and three or four Humvees.

Every truck and every Humvee had some type of homemade armor on it. Rough, thick metal plates of rusted steel hung on the doors to protect the driver. Sandbags were in the floor boards to absorb the effects of an explosion from underneath and tired Gunners with dusty scarves and goggles stood up in a hatch on each vehicle. The convoy whipped into the parking area just outside the main operations tent for the transitioning troops, and a sergeant stepped out of a vehicle looking for whoever was in charge. He needed to get us loaded and on the road as fast as possible. This was going to be a quick in-and-out type of event, not much time for anything else.

Seeing all of the makeshift armor, the display of weaponry and the seriousness of the men in the vehicles, someone in our crowd asked the dumb question, "Are we going to get blown up riding in?" The sergeant, obviously tired, red circles around his eyes, his uniform worn and dusty answered with a single, emotionless word, "Maybe." He wasn't joking. It was real, and this was our new reality.

The trip from BIAP to the prison was stressfully uneventful. Cramped into the bed of the truck with duffle bags we traversed small roads, past village-like clusters of homes and onto what was left of a main highway. Little could be seen or visually analyzed from the rectangle canvas opening at the rear of the truck, but the evidence of destruction was visible. Burned out vehicles littered the sides of the road, and damaged sections of highway caused the convoy to zigzag through the maze of war. What little landscape could be seen appeared to be stunted and lifeless especially compared to the tall trees and rolling landscapes I was used to seeing back home.

The convoy slowed and the momentum pushed everyone forward as the driver shifted gears, a noticeable change in the whistle of the engine and then jerking us backwards again, as the driver accelerated to a stopping point. A few of us stuck our heads out beyond the edge of the canvas and could see a heavily sandbagged guard post, presumably an entry control point or ECP. *We must be here*, I thought to myself. I was not exactly sure where *here* was, but I could see that it was a destination. This destination would begin a year long journey for almost everyone with me and it was going to change our lives forever.

Now we kicked the dirt and continued standing around inside the canyon of walls within the FOB. The place was empty of vegetation, just a walled in dust pit with trash to accessorize the Humvee wreckage and air that smelled like a swamp filled with urine.

The greeting that the driver had given us was still fresh in my ears, "Welcome to your new home, this is Abu Ghraib," he had said. I thought to myself, *I don't think this place will ever be home*. A few of the soldiers of the outgoing unit were mingling in with us and introducing themselves, generally just making small talk as we waited for word on where we would stay until some space freed up. The contrasts were obvious. We looked fresh; our uniforms were clean and crisp, we looked rested and none of us wore gloves. We held our water bottles with clean hands rather casually and most of us were not wearing the combat patch on our right sleeve.

The combat patch is a symbol of pride for most soldiers. There was also possibly a little bit of smugness associated with it as well. The Army and all of the other military branches are loaded with badges, ribbons and patches that show proficiency or symbolize some level of elite training. The combat patch is similar and represents the unit a soldier had gone to war with. It is sewn on the right shoulder of the uniform and would usually be accompanied with ribbons on a dress uniform that denotes the same theater of operations. On the Desert Combat Uniforms or

DCUs, a soldier either had or lacked the patch. This symbolism shows a relationship of the individual soldier to a specific unit, and most times, to specific period in history. It says to every other soldier, "I've been there. I've been to war and I came back."

When we were mobilizing at Ft. Dix there was kind of a hierarchy of what people were wearing and what was perceived as importance or as we called it, "Hooah" status. We were anxious to start wearing our DCUs. It meant that we were heading over there, in theater, and everyone who was still wearing the green camouflage wasn't going anywhere anytime soon. After we made it into theater, everyone wanted to get that combat patch sewn on the right shoulder. Most soldiers had this taken care of when they went home on leave. After everyone had a combat patch, then it got narrowed down to which base you were on. Soldiers in the Green Zone in Baghdad somehow had it easier than the soldiers in other places in Iraq or so it was perceived. On each FOB it may have gotten narrowed even further when some soldiers felt that working in the motor pool or in the operations area wasn't combat enough. You had to be out in the open or on a convoy to legitimately make it count. When we all finally got on the plane to come home a year later, the whole notion that someone was better than the other because of a patch became ridiculous. The patch didn't make a soldier and the lack of one didn't take anything away.

The captain and the 1st sergeant came walking back out to where we had been standing and the 1st sergeant called us into formation. "Fall-In," he yelled. And we quickly mustered into a company formation, standing at attention.

"At Ease," the 1st sergeant yelled again and called the platoon sergeants up close to tell them what he had been told. The first squad leader stepped up into platoon's sergeant's place while we stood by, patiently and silently, still studying our new environment.

The platoon sergeants walked back up to take their position, and the 1st sergeant called us back to attention again,

"Attention! Your platoon sergeants will tell you what you need to know and where you can drop your gear. He will also tell you what you will be doing for the next twenty-four hours. Platoon Sergeants . . . take charge!"

Sgt. Breyers turned around and said, "At ease."

He called the platoon in close, informally, and began to give us our most immediate orders, "The building directly behind me is where we will be staying for the next day or two. It is going to be tight for a while, but once the other unit clears out, we'll fill into their spaces. Also, we have to be ready to go to work at 1400 hours today."

"What?" One soldier asked in a surprised tone of voice.

"That's right, we have to go straight to work, and the 1st sergeant had to almost beg to let you get settled in. You have a few hours to find a cot, take a squat, and be out front at 1330 hours with your entire battle rattle. We are getting one shift of turn-over with the other unit and then they are out of here." One by one we affirmed his orders, "Roger that Sergeant Breyers," and we grabbed our bags and moved out.

Our temporary new home was far from accommodating and scant more than an abandoned building. It had some lights that ran off of a generator, and there was a pile of folded army cots in the corner. There was not much in the way of heat and most likely not much in the way of air conditioning either. We pulled the pile of cots apart and began to line them up in a way that got the most people possible in the limited amount of space. There were two side rooms that had been built out with plywood and crude framing that allowed us to stuff in more soldiers. The upstairs area was reserved for females and was a little more spacious due to the substantially smaller number of women in the unit.

I found a minimal amount of square feet in one corner, grabbed a cot, and shoved two of my duffel bags underneath. I stood the other two up against the wall and sat down for a minute just to take it all in. We were here, in Iraq. *I was here*, I thought, and I was not disappointed. I had wanted to be here. I was older, my body ached a little more and I had a civilian career and family back home. I had left a lot behind, but so did everyone else. It looked like I had been dumped in the ass-hole of the world. But, I said to myself, *I wouldn't want it any other way.* I was a soldier and if there was anything left that I wanted to do or accomplish in my military career, this was going to be the time and the place to do it. This felt right for me. I believed I had a level of experience that could be valuable to some of the younger soldiers in a place like this. I was ready to exercise some leadership and do as much as I could do, there was no holding back. I was sorry that the deployment had upset my family and especially my wife, but I had to be here.

I hadn't served with any of these men or women before, and we didn't have a lot of "get to know you" time while we were mobilizing at Ft. Dix. Time spent on the ranges and standing in lines offered some opportunities to become friends, but on a limited basis. In some ways the unfamiliarity was a good thing. There were no preconceptions to overcome on my part and everyone got the same chance to prove him or herself, for better or for worse. After I had gotten to know some of the men and women in the unit, I believed that almost all of them to be good people and good soldiers; willing to work hard and take care of each other. There are always a few strange ducks in the mix, but I was not in a position to judge anyone and I may have seemed strange to them as well. It would be during the next twelve to fifteen months that the real friendships would be made, and the real mettle would be tested.

At 1330 hours, one half of first platoon mustered in the area between the buildings. After a quick briefing by Sergeant Breyers on what we should be doing for the remainder of the day and what would became our shift, we moved out to go to work. We walked past partially destroyed buildings and piles of debris and trash that had blown against the fence line. Many of the buildings had murals painted on them of Saddam Hussein in uniform and posed in some sort of stoic or heroic manner that evoked the idea of an intrepid warrior leading his men across the battlefield to victory. It reminded me of the propaganda posters of Hitler or Mussolini during World War II, and it was easy to see that maybe Saddam Hussein had copied some of the style, if not the emotional suggestion of the two dictators.

Out through a set of chain-link fence gates, was the main outside prison compound known as Ganci. It was broken into eight separate camps and divided by a rough dirt road with four camps on each side. The numbering of the camps was like the grid pattern of city blocks with even numbers on the right and odd numbers on the left. First platoon was assigned Ganci 1 and Ganci 2 and we divided into two groups or shifts; one was going to pick up the day shift from noon to midnight and the other from midnight to noon.

Each camp was centered around a medium sized army tent set up as the command post (CP) that was partially sandbagged on all sides with a main door and a large plexi-glass window on one corner. It was nothing fancy, but it was going to be home half of my day, at least for the time being. Inside, it had an arrangement of field desks set up for the log book and a table for the radio. A small refrigerator and a few chairs provided some creature comforts. Most CPs also had a small oil fired heater in the center that was brought in for the winter months. It was adequate for the mission, but neither comfortable nor uncomfortable.

Triple strands of razor wire surrounded the perimeter, and soldiers who paced the perimeter watched us curiously. I am sure they knew we were their relief. I told myself, *I know they're glad we're here.* The Guard towers were located on the sides of the camp, spaced halfway between the corners and were nothing more than simple plywood boxes, sandbagged and sitting on top of metal shipping containers. Each tower was manned with at least one soldier and typically one tower at each camp had a machine gun located in it.

Behind the wire was our mission, hundreds of men captured on the battlefield at the outset of the war or in subsequent raids or fighting in Iraq. The raids in villages and towns were designed to reduce the increasing number of attacks taking place on coalition forces. These attacks were starting to tally up in terms of blood spilled and lives lost. These men, our enemy, were pacing the inside perimeter of the wire and they too watched us curiously. Most were wearing thawbs, traditional Arab clothing we called man dresses, a fashion style that was not familiar to us in the United States. Most soldiers found the attire odd, but understood the cultural aspect and cared little about what they wore. Some dressed with the more conventional clothing of pants and a shirt, but all appeared to be dirty and some tattered. Our enemy also spanned a complete range of age and social-economic groups from very old to very young, possibly wealthy, poor, educated and more than likely, uneducated. It seemed that no one was exempt. Many looked as if they had not bathed in several days and were unshaven while others carried the visible scars of war on their bodies. Honestly, it was hard to see our enemy in their faces or understand the malice of their nature, but the fact that we were here was evidence that it existed and the propaganda machine of the mass media ensured us that they were the enemy.

Milk Run

THE DAYS, WEEKS AND MONTHS passed quickly and slowly at the same time: we woke up each day knowing that we were a day closer to going home, but we also knew we still had a sizeable job ahead of us. In a little more than nine months after arriving, the mission of the battalion had expanded and more was being required. There was the addition of family visitations for detainees, regular sick calls at each camp, and visits from the Red Crescent or other humanitarian organizations. An increasing prisoner population meant simple tasks such as feeding them and allowing them to bathe took longer and consumed more time out of each day. We also handed out all of the necessities of comfortable confinement; i.e. toothpaste, sandals, clothes, prayer rugs, Korans and battery-less radios, just to name a few. Additionally, our manpower had shrunk, and our enemy had become more deadly and more efficient in their fight against what they saw as an occupation. The Army was also making constant changes to the prison in the ways of new construction and an operational structure that increasingly resembled what could be recognized in a stateside penitentiary. All of this was being accomplished while situated in a forward battle area under regular and constant attacks from insurgent forces. The most notable was the Mahdi Army, an Iraqi paramilitary force formed specifically to fight against coalition forces in Iraq. As the missions reshaped themselves or morphed, we also adapted and changed with them. Long hours were the norm, remaining flexible was crucial, and uncertainty was a given. For some reason it didn't seemed to bother everyone. We got tired and the days seem like they were never going to end, but we had hardened right along with the mission and developed a good working rhythm. It was also, as they say, all in a day's work.

Staff Sergeant Arron Osborne, Sergeant Geoff Gerhard and I had found ourselves packaged together as a team and we had been picking up a lot of the air escort missions or convoys that left FOB on a regularly basis. We had struck a provisional deal with our operations NCO, Sergeant 1st class Groomes, a little more than six weeks beforehand and for the most part he had held up his end of the bargain. We had simply asked that as we get closer to going home we wanted the trips to taper down. Sergeant Groomes or "Yard Dog" as he was known had agreed, but what was designated as our final mission had taken place for the third time; we couldn't exactly quit when we wanted to quit. He was unquestionably short on people and he needed us to keep going out to almost the very end of our tour or at least until he could get enough replacements on the ground to pick up the missions. Sgt. Groomes was a stout African-American man with a deep voice, who had seen his share of deployments. He was a veteran of the first Gulf War and had done a tour in Kosovo. Enormously experienced, he had the responsibility as the company operations sergeant to make the most of his people,. He adjusted resources as necessary, and put out whatever fire was hottest at the time. The name "Yard Dog" seemed to fit because he was everywhere, all the time; he never seemed to sleep.

One dreary afternoon, we pulled Sgt. Groomes aside under a concrete canopy before he could run off, and laid out a conceptual plan for him, a provisional deal. It was an idea that went against a time honored golden rule of being in the military—never volunteer. Regardless, the three of us saw a problem we thought we could help solve and thought maybe there would be something in it for us. Every time a flight was scheduled, Sgt. Groomes had to scramble around to find people who could make it. For the most part, it was the same routine over and over. Round up available soldiers, search prisoners, and escort prisoners on either too hot or too cold plane rides or equally uncomfortable convoys. Deliver detainees to another location, typically spend the night somewhere, and finally hop a ride back to Abu. I often referred to them as "milk runs." Detainee relocation was not exactly boring, but it was predictably uncomfortable, sometimes stressful, and long. The deployment was going to be winding down in the next few months, and the holidays were approaching. Fewer and fewer soldiers wanted to be traveling outside the wall and most were already busy. Yanking them away would leave a hole in a squad leader's schedule that wasn't easily filled. Gerhard, Osborne, also known as Oz, and I worked with the In-Processing and Holding Area, or IHA. We were also running a prisoner education program initiated at the request of General Miller and passed down to the three of us. It made little sense at the time, but this unusual program allowed us to set our own schedule to a certain degree. This aspect, combined with the job at the IHA or working in the camps gave us some flexibility.

"We have an idea for you to consider," I said to Sgt. Groomes,

"I'm listening," he replied and pulled his sunglasses down around his neck.

"You need MPs whenever you move prisoners around, right?"

Sgt. Groomes nodded, shifted his feet, and peered over his glasses.

"And sometimes you're scrambling around trying to find a few people to go just before the flight is ready to leave, right?"

"You're right," he said.

"Well . . .Oz, Gerhard and I will pick up all of the air missions so you won't have to screw around with chasing people down every time you need to send someone off. We'll keep our bag packed, and all you have to do is find me and give us a time to be at the landing pad."

"This is an interesting concept, Sgt. Wasserman. Would you guys also be good for a few convoys, if I need you?"

"Of course, Sgt. Groomes, we're here for you," I said smiling back at him.

"Well, let me give it some thought, but be careful what you ask for, Sgt. Wasserman," he replied, " you just might get it."

A few days later, he took us up on our offer and over the next few weeks Oz, Gerhard and I, along with several more soldiers were flying out at regular intervals or were being tasked with convoys making regular runs to the hospitals in the Green Zone or Balad. This continued through the holidays and at one point Sgt. Groomes joked that he was going to get us a set of aircrew wings to wear on our uniforms.

Sometime after Christmas Sgt. Groomes pulled Oz and me for another trip to Balad and told us again that it could be our last trip outside the wire. Again, he wanted us to escort a few prisoners to the hospital, drop them off, and fly back the next day. Easy enough, we thought. We knew how the mission would unfold. All we really needed was a departure time and the number of detainees we would be escorting.

Early evening came and it was already dark outside. I yanked my backpack up onto one shoulder, grabbed my weapon and my helmet, and closed the narrow metal door to my room. I walked down the concrete steps and navigated a dimly lit hallway to Osborne's door. The slightest tapping with my knuckles was amplified like a Chinese gong.

"Are you ready, Oz?' I asked, as I pulled the squeaking door open.

"Yeah, just let me grab a bottle of water, and I'm good," Oz replied.

"Groomes said we needed to be on the flight line by 1900 hours, and its right at 1845 now," I said, trying to add a sense of urgency to get him moving a little faster.

Oz pulled up his pack, grabbed his weapon, and helmet, and I closed his door behind him as we both walked out of our building into the cool evening air of Iraq.

Our boots found the well-worn route that we had trod at least a thousand times before, as if they knew where to go without our having to direct them. It was almost the same path to the chow hall or the operations section and, as it had been to the detention camps before they were relocated to the other side of the FOB. The hard gravel crunched beneath our feet, and the irregular ground was familiar as we approached a large open asphalt pad. You could easily land two Chinooks there with plenty of room to walk around them. Encircling the landing pad was a ribbon of gravel that most likely helped with the drainage when it rained, as infrequent as it was.

We grounded our packs on the gravel area at the edge of the asphalt pad about the same time and a two-and-a-half-ton truck whistled up behind us. An MP climbed down from behind the wheel and another jumped down from the passenger side, and a third MP stood in the back of the open bed with eight detainees in yellow jumpsuits. The detainees had a variety of bandages on different parts of their bodies. A second or two later, a field ambulance stopped alongside the truck. Staff Sergeant Adalwolf, a battalion medic, stepped out and walked to the rear of the ambulance. With a hard twist on the handles, she opened the rear doors and revealed two other wounded Iraqi detainees lying on stretchers, almost certainly a result of the recent fighting taking place in and around Fallujah.

I turned to Oz and said, "It looks like our packages have arrived."

Oz replied, "Yeah, another group of rat bastards getting free medical care at the expense of the U.S Government."

"I hear ya brother," I said with a chuckle, as we each took a knee next to our packs.

"We'll just leave them in the truck until the bird gets here," Oz said. Our destination, Balad, was north of Baghdad on the Tigris River south of Tikrit, the home town of Saddam Hussein. It was also the location of Forward Operating Base, Anaconda, home to both Marine and Army units operating in the area north of Baghdad. It had all of the trappings of state side bases with Pizza Huts, Burger Kings and numerous small Haji markets selling anything from pirated DVDs to fine gold jewelry.

Whatever niceties Anaconda had available meant little to Osborne and me on this particular evening. It had only one thing that we needed; a field hospital. Our mission was to escort the wounded prisoners to the hospital where they could receive a higher level of care than could be provided at Abu Ghraib.

"I talked with my son, Kyle, the other day," I said, as I switched knees and repositioned my leg, resting my weight against my foot.

"Really, how is he?" Oz asked.

"Good," I said.

"When are you going to talk with him again?"

"I don't know, not tonight, probably when we get back tomorrow. But the last few times I've talked with him, he didn't have much to say. He was more interested in watching his cartoons than talking with me. The one question he asks is when I was coming home, and then he moans and hands the phone off to someone else."

"I'm sure he'll be a lot more excited tomorrow and will probably be more talkative," Oz replied, apparently trying to find some reason an eight-year-old wasn't more phone savvy.

"Maybe," I replied.

Oz supported himself with his weapon as he switched knees and shifted his weight to rest against his pack. He pulled his sleeve back and held his arm up in the residual light from nearby flood lamps to read his watch.

"1930, the helicopters should be here soon," he said. "Yep, this is going to be an easy trip, a milk run. We have ten shot-up hajis and a short flight. We'll drop these guys off at the hospital, hang out somewhere near air operations and catch the first bird back home," I replied with some confidence.

Oz breathed deep and said, "Yeah, it's good to get the hell out of here once in a while."

"I know," I said, "but we'll be wheels up to Kuwait before you know it."

In the distance, we could hear the faint whoop-whoop of helicopter blades cutting through the air. It signaled that the Chinooks were in-bound, and we would be flying out soon. We both stood up and Oz waved over to the MPs standing next to the truck to start getting the detainees ready to load.

The whoop-whoop-whoop got louder as the helicopters circled around low and approached the landing pad with their noses pointed into the wind. We were barely able to make out a dark shape of what looked like a school bus topped with two massive rotors churning the air. Suddenly rhythmic waves of wind began pushing against us as the two Chinooks settled onto the landing pad. We tilted our heads down to block against the fine grains of sand blown at us by the rotor wash. White streaks of light lit up the tips of the blades as they spun through the air and created static electricity from the friction. The pilots geared the engines down as the rear door, locked in a horizontal position as a platform, was slowly lowered to the ground. The aircraft's tail gunner tipped his fifty-caliber machine gun muzzle downward and stood up in an obvious effort to stretch his legs. The crew chief stepped out onto the back deck and gestured in our direction for someone to come over.

I slapped Oz on the shoulder and said, "I got this. Get the group ready."

I broke into a slight jog and double-timed to the rear of the helicopter. I leaned into the crew chief so I could hear what he had to say over the sound of the engines idling above our heads.

He asked, "How many do you have?"

"Ten," I shouted and indicated with my hands a one and a zero.

'Ten plus two?" the crew chief asked, affirming the number of escort personnel.

I nodded in agreement and replied, "Correct, ten plus two."

"Okay, bring them over," he said, I motioned back to Oz to start bringing the prisoners out onto the pad. I walked back, met the entire group about halfway, and shouted to Oz, "Let's load the two litters last, and we'll put four on each side closer to the front."

Oz gave me a thumbs up, and we both began directing the load-on with the other MPs.

It took several minutes to get everyone on board and secured. Oz and I did a head count and verified the number with the records we had been given. Finally, the crew chief, still tethered to the helicopter with his communication cord, leaned into my ear and asked, "Are we good to go?"

I answered, "We're good," and I found a seat closer to the rear of the helicopter. The crew chief whipped his communication cord ahead of him as he stepped back inside the aircraft and grabbed a small remote controller hanging on the bulkhead just inside the door. His thumb found the correct button without searching, and the back deck slowly began to rise back into a level position. Oz had moved to a seat forward of the detainees and sat next to a waist gunner that was typically on each side of the aircraft, just behind the cockpit.

The tail gunner slid back into what looked like a bucket seat from an SUV and got belted back into place. He reached forward with one hand and grabbed the handle of the machine gun while simultaneously giving the crew chief a thumbs up.

At that moment, we were able to hear the engines and rotor blades increase in speed, even through the muffle of our ear protection. The whoop-whoop became a constant roar and I could feel the bonds of gravity break through my feet as the helicopter began to rise and tilted slightly forward. The sensation was similar to that of riding a roller coaster, but without all of the jerking. Within seconds, we could see lights passing below us, and the buildings began to shrink as we gained altitude.

The detainees were secured, and zip ties were placed on their wrists if the nature of their wounds allowed. There was not a lot to do but get comfortable and enjoy the ride. I usually tried to sit in the rear near the open back door. As soon as the Chinook gained a little altitude, the cold air would give way to the residual heat from the engines and the rotor wash whipping it back inside would keep me a little warm. Add a little rocking back and forth, and it had the potential to put me to sleep like a baby in a crib.

In what had become instinctive soldier mode, I wrapped one foot in and around my rifle sling as I pulled it in close between my legs. I slouched back into the cargo net seats and nestled my helmet into a nice supporting notch in the bulkhead. Osborne obviously had not found his sweet spot yet. He had pulled a length of parachute cord from his pack and tied it like a lanyard. As soon as I got comfortable, he walked back to the rear of the aircraft, reached down on my vest and grabbed my D-ring carabineer. He snapped the carabineer onto this homemade lanyard and looped it through the cargo netting, snapping it back onto my vest. I guess he was worried that I was going to fall out.

As he leaned down, I shouted into his ear, "Thanks, honey."

Oz just patted me on the shoulder, walked back to his seat, and nestled in for the remainder of the trip. The next twenty minutes were uneventful as we cruised a few hundred feet off the deck. Oz appeared comfortable and occasionally turned to peer out the side hatch next to him where the waist gunner was located. The detainees were quiet and still. Most had closed their eyes out of either fear or exhaustion. I became relaxed and stared constantly beyond the tail gunner trying to separate the horizon from the dark sky. Occasionally, I reached up, grabbed my cumbersome ballistic vest at the collar and shifted the weight from side to side in an effort to even out the load. I dipped my head just below the top edge of the thick collar, and I could feel the heat of my own body rise up past my face. The smell of dirt and sweat from the past eleven months was not necessarily offensive; it was a badge of hard work and loyal service.

Suddenly, flashes of light bounced through the inside of the aircraft, and the pilot took a swift and deliberate maneuver to evade the spotlights illuminating the helicopters from the ground. I knew instantly, within the half second it took for my brain to process the information what was happening and in that half second I braced for what was going to come next. The helicopter jerked left, pitched up, rolled right, and I could see small, fast zips of light streak past the open back door . . . Tracers! Tracers meant that someone was shooting at us. The fact that I could see them out the back door meant they had missed. If I had been slightly dozing off or in any way cozy in my seat . . . well . . . I was fully awake now. I could feel a tingle run through my spine and all the way down through my feet. Was it fear? No . . . there wasn't enough time to be afraid. It was adrenaline being sloshed around by the forces of gravity. As the helicopter banked left, the tail gunner responded in kind, squeezing off a twenty-round burst. Fire spat out from the end of the barrel in an explosion of force and an orange-white glow invaded the rear deck of the aircraft. The pilot slammed a button in the cockpit, which ejected a series of white-hot flairs that acted as counter measures for possible heat seeking missiles as he banked the helicopter back to the right.

The prisoners were visibly shaken and nervously alert. What little I could see of their faces told me they were scared and justifiably so. All I could do was hang on. I thought, *maybe that lanyard idea of Oz's wasn't so crazy after all.*

I looked at Oz, but could barely read the bland expression on his face. I am sure that it looked similar to mine with one that said, *oh crap; I don't get paid enough for this.* The entire episode was over in less than fifteen or twenty seconds. The aircraft settled back down to smooth flight and it was over. The crew chief did a quick visual check for any possible battle damage. Satisfied that we had not been hit, he sat back down and the next thirty minutes passed uneventfully and quickly.

The change in the engine noise and the pitch of the rotors told us that we were coming in for a landing. Generator powered spotlights on the ground lit up a perimeter around the landing pad as the helicopter slowed down and its nose tilted slightly upward. The rear wheels touched the concrete pad and the weight of the aircraft was absorbed through the shocks as the pilot gently lowered the front end onto its wheels.

The tail gunner unbuckled his seat belt and stood up as I reached down to unclip the carabineer from my vest. I wasn't sure what this thing would have done for me if I had bounced out. It may have dragged me through the air for a while, or it could have just snapped, and I would have fallen out regardless. In any case, it was a nice gesture.

Standing just off the edge of the pad were several medics who had been waiting to receive the wounded prisoners. They walked over to pick up the stretcher-borne detainees first and Oz did a quick head count as a matter of record. The rest were escorted into the hospital and our job was essentially done. We found a small lounge in which to crash for the night and we were awakened early the next morning to catch the first helicopter, a Blackhawk, heading back to Abu.

The flight back was less exciting than the night before. In fact, it was almost refreshingly boring. Maybe it was the few hours of rest or the quick turn-around, but I was feeling good and could see an eventual end to our deployment. Soon the Blackhawk settled on the familiar real estate that we had left the evening before and the rotors began to slow as the engines idled. Off to the side, in the usual waiting area were a group of soldiers I did not recognize. They looked tired and weary, and anyone could tell they understood the mission and the cost. Oz and I grabbed our gear and weapons, jumped out the side door and waved to the pilot as we walked past the cockpit heading for the chow hall to get some fresh eggs and crisp bacon.

"Are we taking today off?" I asked Oz as we walked off the pad.

"We are, and I'll let Groomes know we're back. If you can get up with Gerhard, let him in on the schedule for the next several days."

"Yeah, yeah, no problem. I think we all have to work the camp tomorrow, and then Gerhard and I work and you are off," I explained as we walked.

"Imagine that, I get a laundry day while you guys have to check ass cracks for notes," Oz joked as we strolled back to what had indeed become our home.

As we cleared our weapons and headed into the building, I looked back over my shoulder to see the Blackhawk lifting away with the soldiers seated inside. I wondered what their mission was today. It didn't matter to me, but it did remind me that the job was constant and somebody had to be doing it. I hoped their "milk run" was even more routine than ours had been. However; I did not yet know what was in store for us on our final mission.

Getting the Word

SGT. GROOMES GOT HIS MONEY'S worth from the three of us on convoys and air missions. Gerhard had made a couple trips without Oz or me and had even been on a long road trip to southern Iraq previously. Sgt. Groomes statement, "Be careful what you wish for," proved prophetic as we took numerous excursions to all parts of the country. By early January, we were in the home stretch and we had mentioned to "Yard Dog" that we were less anxious for ventures outside the wall.

One day Gerhard and I were given the simple task of manning the entry control point, better known as the cage or gate, while a massive shakedown of all detainees took place in one of the outside detention camps. The camps made up a larger compound known as Redemption with varying levels of detention. The officer in charge of detainee operations had ordered the search in order to locate and confiscate any makeshift weapons possessed by prisoners and as a routine precaution against escapes. The previous compound, called Ganci, had been torn down, and the new compound was established with eight separate camps that housed a smaller population each. It was located on another section of the 300-plus acres of the prison complex and was near the large septic lake where the "shit sucker" truck emptied. On a day that the wind was blowing in the right direction, the air was, well . . . sweet. Gerhard and I had been inside the camps many times during these shakedowns, and they were anything but standard.

The word "detainee" was used most often instead of the term "prisoner of war" (POW) because of the way the Geneva

Convention defined prisoners of war as opposed to combatants or non-combatants captured on the battlefield. Somewhere along the line, the politicians decided that we needed to use the word "detainee," but it still meant "prisoner." The Iraqi Army had been defeated, and most of the Iraqi soldiers just took off their uniforms, mixed with the civilian population and fought as a guerilla force. This fact, combined with a growing insurgent influence, confused the coalition forces fighting the land battle on the streets about who was friend or foe. For the MPs working the daily grind at the camps, the answer was simple: If they were inside the camps, they were prisoners or detainees; it didn't matter either way. They could not leave.

It was our job to watch the gate, track everyone coming and going and log in all contraband discovered inside. The prison population in Iraq, and probably anywhere in the world, was notorious for having what they were not supposed to have in their possession. In a forward battle area, it could mean life or death for soldiers and detainees alike, if left unchecked. The gate was hardly easy duty, but it was a welcome relief from the searching process. Digging through detainee underwear, leftover food and bedding infested with bugs was anything but fun. Our office for this event consisted of a small green field table set up with two folding chairs, a radio and a notepad. After a few jokes and talk of the latest rumor around camp, which so happened to be the latest dirt on a female soldier who had gotten pregnant, we settled in and were set for the remainder of the day.

Shakedowns required a considerable amount of planning and coordination. Extra personnel were usually brought in to help conduct the search. The Internal Reaction Force, or IRF team, was used to corral and separate the detainees. Extreme control measures were often exercised to prevent a violent uprising while this process was taking place. Prisoners who had already been searched were separated from those who needed to be searched. Sometimes they were restrained with flex-cuffs and in some instances certain detainees were brought out and sent to interrogation. Normally, it took several hours to go through a camp housing 300 to 400 detainees. It was typically a long, hot day, or in winter, just a long day. We didn't know what we would find in the tents that housed the detainees once we got in there. But every nasty thing one could imagine was often stored under mattress pads or hidden away in a variety of creative spaces. Food, kept until it started to rot, was found in pockets dug around the edges of the tents, covered in such a way that made it difficult to locate. That is until you pressed your hand down into it. In some instances, we found cigarettes from which tobacco had been removed and replaced with tightly rolled notes. Since passing of cigarettes among detainees was common, it had become a way to disseminate information that was possibly dangerous to the soldiers.

Osborne, Gerhard and I worked well together as a team and with the constant rearrangement of personnel, we were lucky to have stayed together as we did. However, on this particular day, Sgt. Gerhard and I were in the proverbial "work box" while Osborne had the good fortune of having the day off, or at least one away from the camps. At Abu, you never actually had a day off, since time off of the work schedule was just time to catch up on laundry or to write a letter home. Most times, it meant being pulled for a convoy or some other basic detail, but Oz had gone unnoticed this particular day and stayed mostly in his bunk. As we maintained our post, the Officer in Charge of Detainee Operations walked up with his usual smirk and his good-afternoon greeting. We called him "Captain America" as a play on his real last name, but it was done mostly among the soldiers working in the camps and never in a disrespectful way. That day, however, we called him "Sir."

Captain America could have been a great guy outside the Army, but for the most part he became one of those men that almost everyone loved to hate. No one actually knew why, but when the days got long and the work never seemed to end, it appeared that a common dislike for someone or something acted as a binding element. Today, he was lingering at our post a little longer than usual. Finally, he said, "Guys, would you like to volunteer for a convoy tomorrow?"

There is one thing that a soldier learns early in his military career and that is never to volunteer. It was the golden rule we had broken earlier. Gerhard and I looked at each other for a second. Somehow, I think we could feel it wasn't something we needed to do. So we responded accordingly and declined.

"No, sir, ah, hell no . . . sir."

Captain America just laughed and said, "Sorry, you're going anyway."

We looked at each other again and said, "Yes, sir." Then Gerhard asked, "Where are we going this time, Captain?"

"You're heading south to Bucca," the Captain replied. He then gave us a brief rundown on the mission and said, "You guys will need to get up with Lt. Marana prior to close of business today. He'll tell you what you need to know for tomorrow."

"Roger that, sir," I answered.

There was no need to try to argue about going on this mission, or any mission for that matter. We had asked for the job, and somebody had to go, period. But like everyone else, we were feeling uneasy about any trip when we were so close to going home.

After he left, Gerhard asked, "Why the fuck did he even bother to ask?"

I replied, "I don't know, but let's get out of here and see if we can't finagle Oz into coming along."

We pulled aside two MPs who were searching the tents to take our place at the gate and we were able to end our shift at that moment. We moved out to what the Army called LSA Shadow or Logistical Support Area, Shadow. It was just a fancy name for what we just called "the area." It wasn't much, but we had made the best of it. Sometime around the start of the war, Saddam Hussein had opened the doors of what was left of the prison and pretty much let everyone out hoping they would fight the Americans and avoid an uprising. When the Americans arrived in late 2003, they found an empty, vandalized, broken relic of a prison. As beat up as it was, it was the best detention setup available at the time, and over the course of a year and a half, improvements had been made. We chased out the most of the rats and bats, swept up the dirt, and called it home. It became a thriving little operating base over time, but also a nice, big, static target for mortars. The perimeter was well defended with tall watchtowers and substantially armed Marines. The FOB was not paradise by any stretch of the imagination, but it contained the bare necessities for any ground-pounding Army or Marine unit.

Abu Ghraib had gained infamy in early 2004 with a scandal that hit the world news and jolted the Army with photos of Iraqi prisoners being abused by U.S. soldiers. Our unit was not even in country at the time of the actual incidents, but we had the luck of being the replacement unit for the battalion that had been involved in the incident. Once the depth of the abuse scandal was realized and the investigation was under way, someone had to come in and take over detainee operations. That somebody happened to be us. We were the 391st MP Battalion assigned to the 16th MP Brigade, Airborne. It was rumored that the Army had made a deal with the news media to hold off on the abuse story until the investigation had been completed. I think everyone investigating knew it was going to be explosive and did not want to jeopardize the investigation with a media storm.

By the time the events hit the front page, we had already been in country for two months, and at first it appeared that our units were those involved with these scandals. Nothing could have been further from the truth. In actuality, we were just handed the mop and asked to clean up the mess. By early April, our own families watching the news reports at home were questioning us about what they were hearing and seeing on TV. We knew very little about what was being broadcast to the world, but we were beginning to feel the impact in the way of retaliatory mortar and rocket attacks against the prison. The allegations added fuel to an already raging fire of disappointment and anger from what the Iraqi people were beginning to see as an occupation. Insurgent attacks had also increased as the politicians struggled to establish a new government, a government free of Saddam Hussein.

Gerhard and I met up with Lt. Marana later that evening and got the whole scoop on the mission. We were to rally at 0600 hours just outside the operations area with two other Humvees and six additional soldiers, then travel to southern Iraq by convoy to pick up seventeen or eighteen detainees being held at camp Bucca. The detainees were to be transported in commercial buses, contracted from Iraqi locals, which were supposed to be waiting for us the next morning.

The Lieutenant explained the obvious. "Bring all of your ammo, all of your weapons, try to get a SAW and prepare to spend the night. The two of you will ride back with the detainees on the bus and maintain security." The SAW was a squad automatic weapon or, in laymen's terms, a machine gun. Most of the Humvees that traveled in convoys had a SAW or .50

caliber mounted on the top, with a gunner in the turret. This was a vehicle's main protection during attacks on the road, but it always exposed the gunner to hostile fire.

So far, the assignment sounded like loads of fun. Gerhard and I were thinking the same thing, *twelve hours in a bus with a bunch of Hajis who hated our guts, had probably killed Americans and had not bathed in a week.* Gerhard even questioned why we needed to go on this death march in the first place. Why not just stuff them in a couple helicopters and fly them here in a few hours? What the hell happened to that idea?

Camp Bucca was another major detention facility located in Iraq. Because it was in the southernmost region near the Kuwaiti border, it was rarely attacked heavily, at least at this point in the war, and it offered a few more amenities to the soldiers. However, the soft soil conditions made the threat of escape through tunneling greater. At Abu, the ground was rock hard and no one was going to dig through it.

Being on call for Sgt. Groomes to pick up a convoy or a flight had its advantages and disadvantages. Convoys were leaving the FOB every day for one reason or another, but it was usually a regular supply run for the battalion. This gave us a chance to do a little shopping of our own and sometimes a bit of sightseeing in Baghdad. However, prisoner transfers, prisoner pick-ups, or Medevac's also came at regular intervals, and this typically kept us away from the FOB for several days, with few tourist opportunities. These were the bulk of our missions. Osborne had not yet been selected for this specific trip, but, as his buddy, it was my job to convince him that he needed to be with his team. It probably wouldn't take much effort and I was going to guilt him into it one way or the other.

I knocked on Oz's door and heard the groan of my resting friend.

He blurted out, "What?"

"Open the door; have I got a deal for you," I said. A few seconds passed, and then I heard the scratching sound of metal on metal as Oz slid the latch of the former cell door open.

"You'll never guess what Gerhard and I have to do tomorrow."

Oz, who was slightly built, with a twinge of a New York accent and no ability to grow facial hair, except for a pencil thin mustache we called his "porn-stache," gave me an inquisitive look, as if he has just been invited to a hanging, his own.

After a few seconds of letting the question hang in the air, he responded, "Oh, don't hold me in suspense, tell me!"

"Captain America just tagged me and Gerhard for a Bucca trip tomorrow."

"What!" Oz huffed. "Didn't we tell him a week ago that we wanted to stay close to home until we leave? We're way too close to leaving and way too close to getting blown up. I talked with Groomes a few days ago."

"Yes, we did," I said. "But that didn't seem to mean anything. Captain America told us that everyone else is called for, and this one is planned to be overnight."

I asked, almost knowing the answer, "Hey, you want to come? He didn't ask you, but I'm sure he wouldn't give a sweet rat's ass if you went along."

"I don't know," Oz groaned, running his hand through his hair. "Give me a little while to think about it."

"What do you have to do except be lonely all day?" I asked him.

"I don't know," Oz quipped. "I have to shave, finish a word search, do laundry, you know, housework."

We continued to chat for a few moments. We had a quick conversation about our wives, children, and even things of little importance like what the chow hall might try to pass off as food again. Finally, I headed upstairs to commence the routine packing of my gear.

We had our preparation for these trips down to a science. Our pack stayed partially ready most of the time, but it was always good to pull everything out and repack it just to make sure. I would stuff in one set of extra underwear, two pair of socks, a shaving kit, a few chemical lights, a flashlight, a poncho liner to use as a blanket, a little extra food and a few other necessities as the mission dictated. There was also the standard array of our individual military gear, weapons, ammo and any mission specific items. Since I knew we would be escorting detainees, I decided to stop off at supply in the morning and grab a handful of zip-ties. With the exception of weapons, I tried to pack as much as I could into my three-day assault pack. On the outside, I strapped on an extra bottle of water and a small camouflage pillow, which the guys called my "Woobie."

Early into the deployment, I had gone online and purchased the three-day assault pack by Blackhawk, and for the money it gave me the biggest bang for my buck. The assault pack was just a rugged backpack with many smaller attachment straps and pockets that allowed me to add more material and equipment if necessary. I took it on every mission and carried it to work with me every day. It was virtually indestructible and was the single best buy I made while deployed.

About an hour had passed, and I was halfway through the packing and gear check routine when I heard someone knocking on my cell door. "Enter," I bellowed. In walked Oz with an almost "I-can't-believe-this" kind of look on his face. I thought, *I know what you're going to say*. Without any hesitation, he said, "I'm going with you guys."

I did a little prodding and asked him, "Are you sure? Are you sure you don't want to hang back at the camps and feel a few more Haji nuts?" referring to the body searches that took place in the camp every day.

"Oh no, I'm going with you guys." Then Oz said something that is purely characteristic of men that have shared the rigors of combat together or had a bullet split between them a time or two. Oz said, "You know, Wass, the three of us have been together about four months, you and I even longer. In dog years, that's about twenty human years. We go back to Ganci 3. I can't let you guys go without me. We are a team, so let's keep it that way until this is all done."

"I hear you," I said and shook his hand. "I'll see you in the morning."

"Just let the Captain know I am going with you guys," Oz replied.

Ganci was the name given to the detention compound set up at Abu at the very beginning of the war. Ganci 3 was one of eight camps within the compound and was the last camp to remain active from the original Ganci setup. We even nicknamed it "the Alamo." Rumor had it that the Ganci name was given in honor of a fireman who had died at the World Trade Center on 9/11. This gave the place a special meaning and reminded us why we were there. A person would also have to understand that three or four months over there was more or less a lifetime in the normal world. Friendships were built in a day knowing they were going to end in less than a week when the mission changed. If you were able to work with someone for the better part of your tour and able to get along with them, it was a gift.

A few minutes later, I walked over to the company TOC and bumped into Sgt. Brown on the way, a soldier from one of our sister companies in the battalion. Sgt. Brown and I were from the same area back in the States and knew some of the same people. We had spoken before, and I liked Brown. I actually thought he was a pretty cool soldier. He had a good attitude and was eager to do the job. On this particular evening, he told me that he was also going to be riding with us on the mission.

"Did Captain America catch up with you, too?" I asked.

"Yep," he replied, and he said that he wanted to be in the turret tomorrow.

"Hey, it makes no difference to me. Oz is going, too. Personally, I think the Captain would like to get rid of all three of us for a few days," I told him.

Brown asked, "Why does Os want to go to Bucca? It is a long-ass trip."

I said, "Oh, partly because we've done so many missions together that he would feel left out if he wasn't with us on this one and partly because it's two days away from here."

"I know what you're saying. Hey, I'll see ya in the morning," he said, and I continued to walk toward the TOC to tell the Captain of Oz's decision. He may have had something planned that wouldn't allow Oz to tag along, but more than likely this was not going to be the case. Regardless, it was always a good idea to keep the chain of command in the loop.

I don't remember who was working the Charge of Quarters or CQ desk at the time, but I let the soldier on duty know that Sgt. Osborne and I would be headed to camp Bucca, and we would be gone for two days. They seemed to have already had this information, and I think a list was already passed on to the company commander. The single addition was Osborne's name. On my way out, the Captain was on his way in, and I told him that Oz wanted to go with us, reaffirming that it was okay with him.

He asked, "Why?" Then, before I could answer, he said, "I don't care. If he wants to go, its fine with me—just let Lt. Bodiker know."

Lt. Bodiker was also from our company and would be the convoy commander. Lt. Bodiker was short and muscular; you could easily tell he spent his free time in the gym. He kept a low profile and did his job well; his duties kept him inside a building most of the time, and some soldiers felt that he had lost touch with the soldiers in the camps. Ironically, his position inside also made him available for more than the average number of convoys. That in itself is admirable. He, along with Spc. Gillman, had certainly dodged more IEDs than anyone else in the company and managed not to get blown up doing it. Gillman and Bodiker would pair up with Sgt. Garner as the turret gunner and fill a Humvee for this trip.

It had been dark for a while, and most everyone who was not working was tired. A few guys sat under a camouflage net on a makeshift patio and smoked cigars. I gave the guys sitting outside a wave as I walked up the stairs. I grabbed my shaving kit, towel and headed back downstairs to take a shower. Afterwards, I would make a phone call to my wife and then turn in for the evening. I needed to relax and clear my head so that I could get to sleep and be ready for the long ride the next day.

Whatever it took, we all needed something to wrap up our day before trying to get to sleep. Everyone needed that mental relief valve that allowed a level of tension to be unloaded. As for me, I enjoyed lying in my bunk with a set of headphones and small CD player that Nadaleane had given me before I deployed. I lay there staring up at a rusty metal hook that was cemented into the ceiling. I wondered almost nightly what that hook was for. I thought I knew; maybe I did. But how did it rust inside a building in a desert? I placed the CD player on my chest and slid the earphones over my head. I had a nice variety of music, but I was in a phase where I particularly enjoyed some of the older Tom Jones songs. I leaned back, reached over my head and turned out the light. I stared back up at the ceiling again, but I could not see the hook. My index finger found the play button and another finger hit the skip button until I found "Delilah", a song that suited my emotions at the moment, and the steady, piercing rhythm began. Good night, sweetie pie, I said to myself, thinking of Nadaleane.

I lay there and let the CD play until my mind forgot where it was or what the day had been, and I drifted off to sleep. The morning would come soon enough.

Moving Out

AT 0530 A FAINT, ANNOYING buzz in my ear dragged me from what otherwise passed for a restful night of sleep and into another undated morning of another unknown day of the week. My hand found the small clock next to my bunk, and I stopped the buzzing. Opening my eyes to almost blackness, I stared at nothing for a second or two and asked myself if I was still in Iraq. I sat up, turned on the light, and if I had any doubt in the haze of waking up, the sparse, but moderately comfortable conditions of my room and my weapon leaning against the wall reassured me that I was where the good Lord had left me the night before.

I slipped my feet into a pair of flip-flops, grabbed my shaving kit and rifle, and headed downstairs for a little personal hygiene time. I had decided a long time ago that I would not carry my ballistic vest or helmet with me when I decided to shit, shower and shave. I figured that if they got me during those important thirty minutes that I took for myself each day, then, what the hell, they win.

As I stepped away from the security of the doorway, I could see the glow of a rising sun behind a building to my east. It was still mostly dark, chilly and quiet. I paused for a second and walked over to the corner of my building to lean my rifle against the wall. I tucked my shaving kit under my arm and began to take a piss. Since New Year's Day, I had made it a point to urinate on the open ground whenever possible. I had rationalized that Iraq had pissed down my back for about eleven months, and I was going to get at least a month to piss on Iraq.

In the center of a horseshoe arrangement of buildings a good twenty-five meters away sat a pair of portable shower trailers. They each had a few shower stalls and sinks and were considered luxurious for a combat zone. A large water tank behind the trailers was filled every other day with purified water brought in by a tanker truck. The used water drained into an underground tank and then was pumped into another truck and dumped into a gray water pond on the other side of the FOB This was an extraordinary effort put forward to give soldiers an opportunity to have a hot shower. The toilets were another story and another thirty-five meters away in a different direction. However, it all seemed primitive compared to the convenience of being home, with having a toilet, shower and sink located within a few feet of the bedroom. I usually took my shower in the evenings after I got off work from the camps or when I came back from missions outside the wall. This morning I needed just enough time to brush my teeth and scrub my face.

At 0600 hours, we strapped on our boots, pulled up our packs, grabbed our weapons and went to work, just as we had done every day for nearly a year. It was January, and the air would hold its briskness until the sun got a little higher in the sky. We were each bundled up in field jackets and individually made our way to an assigned Humvee and began loading our gear. Almost methodically, each soldier had started to prepare for the long mission ahead. Sgt. Gerhard decided that the safest place for him was behind the wheel, so he began the standard preventative maintenance checks on the vehicle, also called PMCS in Army abbreviation language. Sgt. Osborne, who had a background in communications, was checking out the radio and getting frequencies from the convoy commander, Lt. Bodiker. Sgt. Brown, who was trying to track down a mount for the SAW as well as loading ammunition for the mission, occupied the up gunner position. I was going to be acting as a medic for the team. I had loaded my combat lifesaver bag, stocked several liters of water and a few MREs for lunch and possibly dinner on the road. As time began to tick away, it was obvious that the first casualty of the mission was breakfast. I had stuffed some granola bars and beef jerky in my cargo pockets, and I would pass them on to the guys after we hit the road.

Right from the start, we began to encounter a few hiccups in the logistics of the mission. Every trip had its share of minor problems that needed to be solved on the run. But the closer a soldier got to homecoming, the more important the little things became. You might not think that being able to make radio contact with the others was a big deal with as few as three vehicles, but we knew that when, or if, the situation went bad, it would become critical. Gerhard and Oz were struggling to establish communications with the radio to a point that it became annoying for both. Brown could not locate a mount for the SAW and ended up improvising with the bi-pod on the weapon. The details make a difference on any mission, but on long trips, the devil is in the details. Items missed simply increased the opportunity for mistakes that could become the difference between success and failure or life and death.

The best part about this trip was that the farther south we traveled away from Baghdad, the less hostile it became for traveling convoys. Abu Ghraib and Baghdad were located in the notorious Sunni Triangle, an area well known for attacks against coalition forces. The Marines had been in ferocious fights in the Anbar Providence, and we were often caught in the middle. Abu Ghraib's location was also between Baghdad and Fallujah at a major highway intersection. It was kind of a crossroad in hell. It would take approximately an hour before we would clear this region and be able to travel with speed relatively safely.

At 0630, three Humvees left the SP or start point and headed out toward the main gate of Abu Ghraib. Just before exiting the FOB, we stopped at the weapons clearing area and made sure all of our weapons were locked and loaded. The metallic clicking of the charging handle being pulled and released on our rifles was a common sound as convoys entered and departed through the gate. Each click represented a soldier, a weapon, and a round entering its chamber in preparation for a fight, if necessary.

The vehicle's large tires dug into the sandy dirt, kicking up a cloud of dust as the small but swift convoy left the perimeter wall of Abu. The lead Humvee zigzagged through the concrete barriers, turned left onto the hard ball, and headed south on the main supply route toward camp Bucca.

Sitting in the driver's seat was Sgt. Geoff Gerhard. Gerhard was medium height with a stocky build, tank like shoulders and black hair. Even with twelve to fourteen-hour working shifts, he always managed to find time to get to the gym three or four evenings a week for an intense workout. I am sure it was his way of relaxing. Gerhard's finer qualities lay in his courageous attitude, his very proactive approach to prisoner control and his ability to have a little fun while doing his job. On the other hand, he was profane and loud, and he would jump into an argument in the blink of an eye. But we loved him for it, and we knew without question that he was always our friend. We knew a new situation would pop up tomorrow and again test his patience. "Another day in fucking paradise," Gerhard would say.

Gerhard had started the year in the Ganci compound with Osborne and then had moved to prisoner escorts around Abu. After a couple months doing escort duty, Gerhard again switched jobs in the ever changing requirements. One of his new and more prominent duties included maintaining a military police presence for security and separation at the CSH or combat support hospital. Wounded or sick detainees posed the same risk and needed the same security as the ones in the compound. Moreover, high value and high-risk detainees had to be kept away from the general population. While healthy, they were detained in different locations from the majority of the prisoners at Abu Ghraib. In some cases, their leadership influence needed to be quelled to prevent organized disruption among the other detainees. Other times, they were more combative or more dangerous to themselves and thus required the constant monitoring.

There was one detainee that we called Thumby. As the story goes, Thumby was either making an IED or planting an IED when it exploded in his hand. It had blown off all of his fingers on his right hand leaving only his thumb. He looked like a permanent hitchhiker. Thumby would routinely find a sharp piece of metal or fragment of glass and cut himself up until he nearly bled to death. I don't believe he had any real intelligence value, but sooner or later, he was going to kill himself if he was not kept under close surveillance.

We had another detainee we called Jackie Chan. He was actually a high-ranking member of Saddam Hussein's military. For this reason alone, he was separated from the general population, but he was also a fighter. It was evident that he had some martial arts training because every time he was brought out of his confinement cell, he would rare up into a kung fu stance and start fighting the guards. It didn't do him any good, and he would always get put down. Nevertheless, he always went down fighting. To some degree, I almost had to admire his spirit.

According to Gerhard, the most unusual detainee that came through the CSH was one they named "Lucky." He had been a suicide bomber who was supposed to drive a vehicle-borne IED through the wall of the prison complex. The Marines in the towers lit him up before he ever got close, and the car exploded. The explosion blew off one arm that was handcuffed to the steering wheel and one leg. The .50 caliber rounds that shredded the vehicle, also took a sizeable chunk from his head, and the explosion burned 90% of his body. He should have died; however, he didn't and was rightfully named "Lucky." Within a couple of months, he was signaling for food or water, or to let someone know when he needed to go to the bathroom.

In any case, this set of conditions was a perfect fit for someone who enjoyed the yelling as much as Gerhard. It was almost like entertainment for him to work with such a unique cast of characters, but he never let his guard down.

Captain America also happened to be Sgt. Gerhard's company commander. None of us quite figured out why, but there was no love lost between Gerhard and his commander. Oz and I believed that we often caught a little of the leftover heat intended towards Gerhard. In the big picture, it didn't bother us, but we did wonder why. We were all in Ganci together, and we would find a way to take care of each other, regardless, but it sure seemed that there was something more going on than met the eye with Gerhard and his commander.

In the front passenger seat sat Staff Sergeant Arron Osborne. Oz, as we called him. He sat directly over the battery box and on a long trip the batteries would heat up and make it a little uncomfortable to keep your butt in one place. Osborne was from Ohio. He had waited until his mid-thirties to get married and start a family and like me, he had a wife who hated his long absence. Oz had started out in the Ganci camps the day we hit the ground. He mostly worked the midnight shift in the beginning, but with constant rearrangement of personnel, he worked in several of the camps and on both shifts. Oz had endured several riots and a number of small arms and mortar attacks against the prison itself. At one point, he was the Non-Commissioned Officer or NCO in charge at the in-processing center and accounted for the numerous detainees that came and went each day in a constant shuffling process. Together, we had been on countless air missions, or pick-ups, as we called them. We often found ourselves spending the night or chewing the dirt in many different parts of Iraq, much to the chagrin of Command Sergeant Major Vacho and our operations officer, Major Steeple. On one such mission, it took us almost a week to get back, and our operations officer had our last known locations plotted on a mapping board with pushpins. It was like playing a game of "Where's Waldo?" with us. Whenever we got stuck somewhere, I would try to give him a status report with an e-mail or a phone call, and he would just stick a blue pin in the map.

The up gunner in the turret manning the SAW was Sgt. Brown. To me, he resembled Elvis Presley though I doubt he could sing a note to save his life, but he looked like he could. Although he was from Virginia, Brown was cross-leveled to a unit home based in Puerto Rico and had deployed to Iraq with that unit. He was first assigned to the area known as the Hard Site. It was set up like one would expect of a prison in the United States with walls, cells, and cell-blocks, but without the air conditioning, running water and most of the amenities stateside prisons had to offer. It was a living inferno fraught with extreme danger. Because he had spent his time at the Hard Site and not with us in the Ganci compound, he was still the new guy in some respects. He was experienced and had a good reputation as a gunner.

I was sitting in the rear seat behind Oz. I was the old man of the bunch at a year over forty. A few of the younger soldiers called me "Papa Bear." I was also known as the "Wassmonster" and possibly a few less flattering names, but I had sharpened my skills as a combat lifesaver or medic-in-case-you-needed-one while working with the Navy corpsman during the many mortar attacks launched against the FOB. Like Osborne, I started working the first six months in the Ganci compound, had moved to the in-processing center with our squad, and eventually moved to a new compound known as Bison and later called Redemption, once again with Oz and Gerhard. My shift, was usually from noon to midnight in the Ganci compound, and it was during these hours that we faced the majority of our mortar and rocket attacks. I can recall at least twice that my uniform was soaked with blood after treating the wounded and my ears were ringing from the steady absorption of explosions. Quite often, after the sun dipped below the horizon, small arms fire streaked over our heads, accompanied by a rocket propelled grenade or RPG attack.

Like most of us who worked the outside with the detainees, I had become cynical about their honesty and was never sure who was lying and who was not. You couldn't show up to work with personal problems on your mind or be worried about your family and expect to function at one hundred percent. For this reason, we always watched each other's backs and made sure we stayed alert. Nothing was to be taken for granted, especially our safety.

During the long shifts and brief breaks, we would talk about family and what was happening back in the states. It wasn't always good news. Somebody always seemed to be screwing around on someone; money was always disappearing from a checking account; and not everyone got regular mail or had someone to call if they needed help back home. This could be disrupting to a soldier. I had a strong family support system, which allowed me to keep my head in the game with very few distractions to worry about domestically.

I squirmed around in the seat as the convoy sped past small villages and wove its way through destroyed sections of highway or blown-up vehicles. I shoved a box of MREs over to make room for my pack and a softer armrest arrangement. The box reminded me of the many packages that my sister or parents would mail to me. I had given my sister a list of names, and she had started to arrange for packages to be sent to other members in our company who may have not received as many. I was never sure how many she had sent out or to whom they went, but she did tell me that she had received a few letters thanking her for packages. We all looked out for each other, and it wasn't uncommon to spot someone a few dollars if they needed it or to trade your leave slot with someone who needed to go first. A buddy covered his or her buddies' bases unquestionably. Conversely, there had been times in my career I believed that senior NCOs had gone out of their way to be disparaging to soldiers. Here in Iraq, on a deployment that was conceivably going to wrap up my military career when I tried very hard to be a better example to the soldiers around me and end my career on a high note. I did not want people to say, "While I was deployed with him in war, Sgt. Wasserman was an ass."

Oz, Gerhard, and I had also become numb to the rigors of the daily grind. The continuous horrors of the war and the infinite destruction around us had dulled our emotional senses. During the month of April 2004, Abu was effectively under siege, and we had survived several blistering mortar attacks that left dozens killed and several hundred wounded. The main roads out of Abu were becoming littered with burning military vehicles and billowing plumes of black smoke, all a result of insurgent attacks. On March 31, 2004, a convoy carrying four American contractors was attacked in Fallujah, and the spectacle of American bodies being dragged through the streets was shown on television. Had we repeated the Mogadishu mistake? Were we trying to help someone who didn't want it, everyone asked? At a certain point, worrying about it just made it worse. It didn't matter anymore. We were here, and we were going to stay. We could not control when an attack was going to happen, who or what was going to get hit, and when we could be killed. Worrying about our mortality would merely add to an already stressful day that was almost always 100% out of our control. We took every reasonable precaution and believed that we had made the best of challenging circumstances. The rest was a gamble.

What came in over the wall was bad enough, but inside the compound could be just as dangerous. Inside is where we had to focus our concentration. It was sometime during the early months of the deployment while working in the Ganci compound that we learned a valuable lesson about our enemy. The detainees were treacherous and deceitful. If given the chance, they would slit our throats just as easily as they would look at us.

The training and the advice we received told us to be fair, but we also had to be firm. It was constantly reinforced so that the overall handling of the detainees did not breech what the army had decided was proper treatment. Consistency and vigilance were important ingredients in our daily dealings with an ever-growing and hostile prison population. Very simply said, we could not trust the detainees. During a camp shakedown one afternoon, we discovered that a group of prisoners had plans to lure specific guards into the fenced camps and attempt to assassinate them. This was no idle threat, and it brought home the seriousness of our job.

The convoy continued, and a cool breeze swept down through the turret, and the mental movie of our tour began to run in the background in my mind. During the year, the three of us had seen our fair share of games the detainees tried to play to throw us off balance.

On a regular basis the detainees would try to come close tt he razor wire and talk with the soldiers, in more or less a friendly manner. As a conversation ensued, the detainees would bend over the little barbs on the razor wire without notice. If you did enough of them in a selected area, the wire would become ineffective, vulnerable to breach, and we were constantly warning them to stay away from the wire. Often the detainees would try to lead us into conversations about our families, how long we were going to be in Iraq, and other seemingly benign topics. On occasion, when a translator was available to read the notes passed amongst the prisoners, we had discovered small details of those conversations.

We had learned a great deal about their actions and what got them into Abu. We had also gotten to know many of them and learned about their lives under the rule of Saddam Hussein. Almost every day, we caught ourselves thinking of them not as an enemy but just as regular folks, like us, caught up in the war. Maybe they were innocent and were just, as many had said, in their homes when the American soldiers came in and arrested them for no reason. Then again, maybe not.

Of all of the detainees we had in our custody, few stood out enough to make me wonder what would happen to them after we left. But there was one named Omar, better known as "Abu Omar." He spoke fairly good English and even spoke Yugoslavian. Omar actually had a pretty good sense of humor, all things considered. He was a camp chief almost the whole time we worked in the Ganci compound and generally helped keep everything under control. There were many evenings when we were working and the daily grind had slowed down enough when Omar would come to the cage just to talk. I think he just needed the interaction. I have wondered what happened to Omar and if he managed to survive the Iraq that was going to exist.

Most of the time these kinds of talks were not particularly insightful and nothing more than general conversation, but we needed to be careful with our thoughts and with what we discussed. In most cases, we didn't know the whole story behind anyone's capture or the details regarding their detention. We knew some of the detainees had killed soldiers, and almost all of them disliked Americans. Even with seemingly low risk prisoners we had to keep that cautious notion always in the back of our minds. Each of us separately and deliberately had honed our instincts and had a focused emphasis for the mission.

Thinking and Riding

GERHARD, OZ, BROWN, AND I were stuffed into a Humvee roaring down the road toward southern Iraq. I gave a tug on Brown's pant leg to get his attention.

He leaned down though the hatch, "Yeah," he shouted.

"Are you cold?" I asked him.

"No, I'm good."

Gerhard had almost pegged the needle on the speed odometer, and Oz had yet to establish communication with the other two vehicles.

"Don't worry about it, Oz, the damn thing is probably broke," I said lifting my voice loud enough to be heard over the roar of the engine and tires.

Oz was a little perturbed and yelled back to me, "I know, but this is jacked up. We got no convoy brief, no coms to the outside and. . ."

I cut him off to say, "And we have Gerhard driving. We're lucky we're not dead already."

As we headed farther south, the desert seemed to open up and almost invite us into the barren landscape. Unlike the city of Baghdad, the open desert gave us an almost secure feeling because of our ability to see everything around us for miles and miles. I am sure this was mostly an illusion, but after being pinned behind the walls at Abu for the better part of a year and never being able to see who was attacking, the open desert seemed to level the playing field.

In the distance, we saw small earthen huts, tiny figures tending sheep, and an occasional dog running along the side of the road. After about an hour of steady traveling, we caught sight of a whole herd of camels on both sides of the road. I gave Oz a tap on the shoulder and pointed out the window. Oz instinctively reached over to Gerhard, who was focused straight ahead, and pointed off into the distance. Gerhard just laughed. Oz turned around and, in an elevated voice, said, "We've been here an entire year and have never seen a camel until now."

I shouted back, "We don't get out much, and when we do, it's usually in a helicopter, at night—"

Oz interrupted to say, "And usually at two hundred feet off the deck."

Nodding in agreement, a thought came to mind, and I told him, "Let's take a picture so we can finally prove to everyone that we saw a camel."

Oz and I both scrambled through our gear looking for the cameras we usually carried in our pack or cargo pockets. We snapped a few blurry photographs of the open desert and large camel herds as we sped down the road.

After the brief camel excitement was over, we settled down and just tried to get comfortable. The large, all-terrain tires of the Humvee provided a constant, hypnotic roar broken by an occasional word or hand gesture pointing out some new, distant feature in the landscape. Each of us drifted into thoughts of our families and home. I was certain it would be different for each one of us, yet in many ways, it would be the same. What would being home be like, once we got there? What anxieties and uncertainties would we face? We didn't know exactly when, but that day was coming, and this was as good a time as any to start thinking about it.

Gerhard, like most of us, had built up a little intensity over time. He was a man with a great sense of humor, but he said that he felt that his particular brand of humor had bonded with enough hostility to change him. His fuse had gotten shorter. It was hard to tell sometimes if his sarcasm was a joke or anger. Staring straight ahead, he wondered if his wife and kid would know him. Would his family and friends understand all that had happened on the deployment? How deep were some of the images that had been seared into his mind? Over here, he had his friends, and he knew we had his back. At home, could he count on his old friends to do the same? But in reality, how close were we to each other? We might never have become friends if we were not here and forced into depending on one other. All of us were reacting to the situations and the length of time we had been in the country. However, none of us knew what going back to "the real world" would be like after this experience. Hopefully, we would stay in touch.

Soldiers in combat tend to operate at a higher level of alertness and maintain a much higher level of stress for longer periods than the average person. Stress is not necessarily a bad thing. It is the body's way of telling us to be on our toes. If you are in danger, stress tells you to run. If you are being harmed, stress tells you to fight back. It is what psychologists call the flight-or-fight response. Some people do neither and just freeze.

Soldiers, Marines and most members of the military are trained to react appropriately instead of freezing. Assume that the average working man or woman maintains a stress level of three or four on a daily basis, which could sometimes spike to a five or, in extreme cases, to a six. Bad day at work, wife wrecks the car, son gets caught at school with drugs: five or six. Soldiers moving into a combat environment increase an alertness level of about four to ten in a very short period. And ten is maintained for the duration of the deployment or the mission. Soldiers will maintain a high level of alertness until they are at home, in Fort Living Room. A chemical reaction takes place in the body that does not reverse itself immediately. Once home, it can take a long time to go back to a three or four again. For Gerhard and the rest of us, maybe the best we'll ever do is get back down to that calm level of five, the place where the rest of the world is about over the edge and feeling the pressure.

When Gerhard's wife starts getting upset because the dog has crapped on the carpet or the roast was burned, he'll probably just say to himself, *I've seen worse and I've eaten worse. Don't sweat the small stuff.* Ironically enough, he will explode with anger the next time someone slams a carton down on the grocery store counter. All in all, Gerhard will handle his return the way he handled his deployment: with somber stoicism punctuated by moments of intensity. Maybe he will conclude his day in the weight room for an exhausting workout for no other reason than to clear his mind and prepare for the next morning. Coming home would be no different, except that he might not have the support and understanding without his fellow soldiers with him. Gerhard is a solid soldier, but at some point, this hell was going to end. He thought to himself, *How well will I adjust back?* We all wondered the same thing, but for now, it was most important that we stay steady with the mission and focused on the run. We had to get home before we could worry about being there.

In a convoy, it was important for the vehicles to keep the proper distance. Too close, and the vehicles bunched up and became a big, slow-moving target; too far apart and the risk of being cut or separated was a threat. The trick was to maintain your speed and know when to slow down, when to speed up, and when to take a defensive or an aggressive stance. This was why we had Brown in the turret manning the SAW. Brown was our defense.

Gerhard kept his foot to the floor, but once in a while, over the roar of silence, he would lean over and give Oz a solid jolt to the arm. "Wake up, Magoo!" The thump of his fist brought out yelps from Oz, who was concentrating on one of his puzzle books.

"Ouch, that's my playing with myself in the blue canoe arm," he said, referring to the blue colored port-o-johns.

Oz kept a steady supply of word searches, crossword puzzles, and other word decipher books handy. Oz would bury himself in the puzzle books for hours at a time, when we were not scared, bored, or tired. He found some peace solving something in his head. Occasionally, I would tease him and tell him that the one place anything was going to be solved and sound correct was in his mind because nothing he said made any sense.

Today, however, Oz's mind seemed to drift as the desert was opening up to us. He tried once again to bury his thinking in the puzzles, but at every mile, something caught his eye and kept him distracted. Finally, he folded his little paper wad, stuffed it into his backpack, and began staring out the window searching the landscape for friend or foe. At some point, I could see him daydreaming. He'd told me often that he thought of his wife and two-year-old son back in the Midwest. Oz knew his son would have little memory of him being gone, but Oz knew he was gone, and that made him homesick. He said he and his wife had discussed a new bedroom addition to the house. But after living in Iraq in such sparse conditions for such a long time, he questioned whether the addition was important now. Oz's attitude had changed—a once dire crisis was no longer a big issue. The small things could trigger larger, more emotional responses and resentment that may have never existed beforehand. Most combat veterans know that these kinds of issues are often an unseen casualty of war.

On the other hand, Oz said he felt he had contributed something worthy during his tour in Iraq. He had taken on every job that was asked of him, transitioned easily from working the camps for a solid six months to working inside, processing the prisoners, establishing a learning center for the detainees, while working to build a new and somewhat improved set of camps. All the while, he was traveling on numerous convoys and air missions and improvising as the missions reshaped themselves en route. On one trip, Oz and I were transporting a prisoner to the hospital in Baghdad via helicopter when the crew chief gave me the signal to pick up a set of headphones. He asked if the prisoner was stable. I had become the default flight medic on this otherwise routine day, and I gave the crew chief the thumbs up, indicating that he was stable. The crew chief said that we needed to make a little detour, and the next thing I knew, we were landing at another FOB to pick up an injured soldier who also needed to get to the hospital as soon as possible. Suddenly, we had two people we had to worry about. In addition, we were the security for the helicopter while it was on the ground with blades turning. The paradox of this picture was that we had an American soldier lying next to an Iraqi prisoner as we flew them both to the hospital.

Oz had signed up when the Army slogan was "Be all that you can be." In his heart, he knew the Army had gotten what they needed from him. At the very least, he could look at himself in the mirror and know that he had done everything he was asked to do and left nothing on the table to regret.

In more than one attack on Abu Ghraib, Oz had distinguished himself by maintaining his post while helping to keep hundreds of prisoners inside a thin strand of wire that separated a whole bunch of them from not so many of us. What we simply called the wire was actually three strands of razor wire stacked like a pyramid about five to six feet high. Sometimes, it felt like running through hell with gasoline soaked underwear was easier than standing your ground on the wire during a full-scale riot combined with an outside attack on the prison. The possibility of their breaching that wire was real and was always a major concern to the MPs that walked the perimeter every day.

The name Abu Ghraib carried a notorious meaning and brought a different kind of concern to the Iraqi people, It had served as Saddam's torture and execution prison. We knew that *Abu* meant, "Father of." However, the etymology of the word *Ghraib*, which is sometimes spelled *Ghuraab*, was more difficult to track and could have a variety of meanings, depending on how the word was spelled. One spelling indicated some derivative of the words "strange," "stranger," or "strangeness." Another spelling meant "departed, banished, or pushed away," and yet another spelling alluded to birds or crows. In many Arabic cultures, when a person is accused of a crime and sent to prison, it brings shame on the family. That person is banished from the family or becomes a stranger to the family. The best interpretation or best guess of the meaning of Abu Ghraib is "Father of the Banished" or "Father of the Stranger." This would make perfect sense, but it did not appear that even the Iraqi people knew the correct pronunciation. They did, however, fear the reputation and knew they didn't want to be inside Abu Ghraib.

In a barren corner of the Abu Ghraib prison perimeter, the Ganci compound was hastily constructed at the outset of the war. It soon became evident that a larger prison was going to become necessary as more and more combatants were captured in attacks against coalition forces. The outside detention area was a fraction of the almost three hundred acres inside the perimeter wall and was never planned as the long-term solution. The compound itself was broken into eight separate camps, and each camp had approximately a dozen large tents with dirt floors that housed three hundred to five hundred detainees. The compound, as it turned out, was constructed on an old landfill. It contained everything from broken pieces of concrete to steel reinforcing bar and even buried explosives. During a riot, all of that debris was dug up, turned into homemade weapons and flung at us. Usually, this would happen during a coordinated attack from outside the wall. The main protection was the thin strand of razor wire, your buddies, your body armor, and your training.

We had been there all too often, and on this trip, our thoughts would take us there again. A twelve-hour road trip will give a person a lot of time to do nothing but think. We wondered if our experiences would ever leave us when we left Iraq. Would we even want them to? Could we maintain this composure once we were back at our old jobs?

Working the Ganci compound was the gravel-in-your-gut, rock-busting duty at Abu. It was also most crucial; it was the mission. At one point, we had nearly 8,000 detainees and three quarters of them were held in the compounds in the outside camps, either Ganci or Redemption. The MPs job required constant vigilance. The detainees continuously tried to plan and execute escapes. Manipulation or distraction of the guards was ongoing and was a key element in the detainee's goal of freedom. Every item was a potential weapon. Every conversation was an opportunity for the Hajis to gain some intelligence to aid them in an escape or to overthrow the camp at some point. To make matters worse, the region has blistering heat in the summer, when temperatures typically reached 135 degrees at mid-day. A soldier could not drink enough water in July to stay hydrated. A twelve-hour workday was typical. Add an hour or so at each end for a little prep or debrief, and it added up to a long, hot day, working with several thousand dangerous human beings as your new friends. Because we were trained soldiers and became conditioned to this work environment we could meet these challenges. There was no one better suited for the job.

Oz bowed his head and rested it in his thumb and forefinger, while rubbing his eyes. Slowly he closed his eyes for thirty seconds of rest. Within a moment or two, he raised his head again, sat up straight, and stared out the window, scanning the landscape. His mind was taking him back to one of the many attacks we had just a few weeks before. In December of 2004, Oz had just laid his head down for a brief nap after returning from a one-day mission. Everyone was moving about and heading to evening chow. Then Wham! Wham! Thump! . . . Wham! The sound was deafening, and there was little doubt what it was. Mortars! The sound was overwhelming as if it were just yards away from the building. The percussion waves of the explosion vibrated the building and jarred the ground like an earthquake. Oz sat up straight in his bed and flung his door open. In the security of the concrete building, a person was relatively safe. Outside, during a mortar attack, we were just soft tissue exposed to jagged, hot metal flying at the speed of a bullet.

Immediately Oz could hear cries for help. The mortar rounds had landed just yards away from our building, just inside our LSA near the shower trailers. This area was usually active with soldiers during the late afternoon, and it was within twenty to thirty feet from where Oz was lying in his room. Smoke from exploded rounds filled the air like thick fog as he and other soldiers ran to aid the wounded men crying for help. Another soldier, Sgt. Brickline, and Oz found a man from a sister company lying on the ground severely wounded. The explosion had caught him completely off guard as he walked to the shower and several large pieces of shrapnel had torn into him. He had blood pouring from his side and chest. Oz could hear the labored sucking sound of air from the chest wound and could see that a piece of jagged metal had torn into his lower abdomen and had most certainly damaged some internal organs. Oz grabbed a T-shirt and attempted to stop the bleeding as Brickline ran to get a Humvee. There wasn't any time to wait for an ambulance or the medics; he needed to go to the field hospital right then and there. Brickline wheeled around in the Humvee as Oz covered and applied direct pressure to the chest wound and packed the abdominal wound as best as he could. Together, they hoisted him over the back seat and laid him out in the flat area between the seats, extending his legs towards the rear of the truck.

Sgt. Brickline jumped into the driver's seat as Oz dove in through the rear passenger door. He continued to apply direct pressure over the wound, while constantly talking to the soldier and saying, "It's not that bad; you're going to be fine." Brickline dodged the potholes in the rough road as he sped towards the field hospital. The sound of the Humvee engine winding up and the dust trail that followed was barely noticed as soldiers scrambled to help the others wounded in the same attack.

Within a minute or two, Sgt. Brickline had pulled up to the CSH and had backed up to the main door. He jumped out and started calling for help. Several medics and nurses stood just inside the door, unaware that any U.S. Soldiers had been hit. They ran out and immediately began to lift the wounded man from the vehicle and onto a stretcher. The hospital came alive with a flurry of activity as more wounded arrived and triage began.

Oz's mind was now racing and the adrenaline was pumping. He and Sgt. Brickline could hardly believe what just had happened. They jumped back into the vehicle and raced back towards the LSA. Oz looked down at his hands and arms and saw they were covered in blood; his pants were soaked, kneeling over the man in the bed of the Humvee.

Inside the open horseshoe of the LSA, a flurry of activity continued. The wounded soldiers, six in all were being evacuated to the field hospital. Bloodied bandages, gauze wrappers, and the remnants of discarded IV sets littered the ground. All of the wounded soldiers survived the attack and four of the soldiers with less serious wounds remained at Abu until they could return to duty. The two more seriously wounded soldiers were evacuated to Germany for more extensive treatment and eventually were shipped back to the states for long-term treatment and rehabilitation.

Oz and Sgt. Brickline parked the Humvee and stepped out into the area now clear of smoke. They talked with another group of soldiers and began to recap the attack that had just taken place. "The Hajis finally did it," Oz said. "They finally hit us right where we live." Mortar rounds had gotten close before, but up until then, none had hit directly inside what was generally considered a safe zone inside the LSA. As they talked and looked around, they discovered yet another horror or blessing— unexploded ordnance. Ten rounds had landed, but only five had actually exploded. That left five unexploded rounds lying on the ground in the immediate vicinity. The prospect of what could have happened was as frightening, maybe even more so, than what had already happened.

Suddenly, our Humvee hit a pothole in the road that jolted Oz back to the reality of the here and now. This reality was our mission on this day and our rational insanity, until we left Iraq.

Somehow, Oz had managed to keep his head together for the year or so of this deployment by finding humor in the madness. What was normal here would be quite unacceptable once we got back to the civilized world and he knew it. The tasteless jokes with our buddies, told while pulling our shifts in Iraq, would more than likely get us fired from civilian jobs. The emotionless descriptions of all that we had seen would not be acceptable with our in-laws at dinner.

At this point, we had been on the road for several hours, and the gunner in the Humvee ahead of us gave a hand signal that we were approaching a traffic control point. During the morning drive, Gerhard and Osborne had played and tweaked with the radio enough that they were eventually able to establish communication between the vehicles. Loudly crackling across the speaker, a voice broke the silence, "Shadow Guard, this is Shadow Move."

Oz grabbed the microphone, "Shadow Move, this is Shadow Guard. Go ahead."

"Shadow Guard, be advised that we will approach POL point in about ten mikes. How copy over?" the voice said.

"Roger, POL point in ten . . . Shadow Guard out." Oz tossed the microphone back on top of the radio, turned around to me and asked, "Did you get that?"

I nodded and yanked Brown's pants leg to get his attention.

Bundled with a checked scarf similar to those worn by the Israeli army, his eyes covered with sand goggles, Brown bent down and got his head within listening range.

"Yeah?" he asked. I told him, "We're stopping in about ten . . . . fuel, food, and potty break." Brown gave me the thumbs up and stood back up in the turret.

Within a few minutes, the vehicles began to slow down, and there was a noticeable change in the pitch of the engine noise. The roar of the tires lessened as the Humvee reduced speed. We were a little better than halfway to our destination, and we were ready to stretch our legs. There is not much legroom in a

Humvee for a tall person, and it can be especially uncomfortable on long rides.

The tall, gray, sand-filled Hesco barriers came into view, and the zigzag motion of the Humvee indicated that we were close to the fuel point. Gerhard began to drive as if he were competing in the Grand Prix, pulling the Humvee right and left as he slowed and then stopped at the weapons clearing area. Again, the clicking of metal on metal was heard as we cleared our weapons and then moved forward. Finally, the convoy stopped, and it gave us the chance to take a well-deserved break.

We let out a collective sigh as the doors were flung open, and we began to unfold our stiff legs and stretch our frozen bodies from inside the vehicle. By then, the sun was high in the sky, but a respectable chill was still in the air. We began to move around within the security of gray Hesco barriers as the first vehicle began fueling up. While we waited, it was a good time to visit the latrine, get rid of the trash, and grab a bite to eat. Oz threw some MREs on the hood and asked, "Any of you dog faces hungry?" In true John Wayne fashion, Gerhard pulled off his vest and helmet and threw them over the door of the vehicle. We all followed suit and were relieved to have a few moments unburdened of the protective weight. Being this far south in Iraq, and especially several hours away from the Sunni Triangle region, gave us a small feeling of safety. Again, I think it was something about being able to see in every direction for miles and have the advantageous of forewarning that added a sense of safety or at least of being less vulnerable. I grabbed a spaghetti meal, poured some water into the chemical heater packet, and began to warm up lunch, at least for the thousandth time. MREs stood for Meals Ready to Eat. They were prepared packages of 2000-calorie meals that would last in storage for years. We used to say that when everything else on earth was destroyed, all that was going to be left would be cockroaches and MREs. Since the dawn of warfare, the question that always needed an answer was how to feed an army deployed and on the move. The MRE was the Army's 21st century answer. The spaghetti meal, in my opinion, is the most edible of MREs meals, along with chili-mac and generally almost anything with tomato sauce. Maybe it is the tomato sauce or the fact that canned spaghetti and Spaghetti-O's were not all that bad when we were kids. Some of the meals had an acquired taste or, in other words, they were nasty, and we would have to be pretty damn hungry to want to eat them.

All four of us were outside the Humvee breathing in the fresh air and waiting our turn to move forward to take on fuel. Oz jumped in the driver's seat and edged the vehicle up while we continued our picnic on the hood. By then, everyone in the convoy was moving around within the tiny fortress of the POL point. Brown jumped up on the rear of the vehicle ahead of us and snapped a picture with one of those Kodak throwaway cameras. Oz shouted, "Hey, great idea!" He tossed Brown his digital camera for one or two quick shots he could save for himself. I began to tell Gerhard and Oz that this trip had not turned out all that bad after all and maybe we deserved a holiday. It had been a busy year, and every once in a while, even ugly guys like us get a break in life.

The first Humvee rolled forward, and I drove our vehicle up a few meters. Everyone still had food lying on the hood and was walking slowly beside the Humvee as I moved to the fuel hose, stopped, and pulled up the parking brake. A specialist working the pump attached a grounding wire to the body of the truck and started pumping in the diesel. In the meantime, we continued to enjoy the breather, not just a breather outside the vehicle, but also away from Abu and mostly from the constant strain of the combat environment.

Since the day we hit the ground, we had had some type of attack on the FOB nearly every day. The most devastating attacks had come from the intense mortar fire. On several occasions, we had sustained ten or twelve dead and over ninety detainees wounded in a single attack. If not mortars, we had our share of RPG attacks, small arms fire, vehicle-driven bombs, and just for fun, a combined coordinated attack of them all. How our unit was able to keep the madness to a minimum, God only knows.

The specialist pulled the nozzle from the gas tank and said, "You're topped off." Gerhard jumped in, started her up, and pulled ahead twenty yards or so, and the trail vehicle moved into place. We began to clear the remaining lunch trash and did a quick weapons check. Even if they were clean, it never hurt to wipe our weapons down and check our ammo. It may have seemed redundant, but it reinforced muscle memory to always to know every square centimeter of our weapons and how to get to our ammo, even in the dark. Oz, Gerhard, and I were also packing our backpacks in a similar manner and constantly re-familiarized each other with the gear that we were carrying. Oz often said, "When the feces hits the rotary device," all thinking goes out the window, and all we had to fall back on was our training. The things that we had trained on a million boring times would be that which would save us.

Before too long, Lt. Bodiker walked by, heading toward the lead vehicle, and told us to be ready in ten. He also told us that we would be stopping at the Ruins of Ur for a brief sightseeing visit.

I looked at Oz and said, "That's cool?"

Oz replied, with a kind of a question mark on his face, "Very cool . . . What is Ur?"

I looked at him and said, "Ur, in the Bible, Ur. I believe it's the home of Abraham."

Oz just put on his helmet and said, "Really? Sounds cool, I guess. Now we get a vacation? Twelve months in the sandbox, and we finally get to go sightseeing."

Ur was the historical birthplace of Abraham mentioned in the Old Testament of the Bible. It was also an archeological site, but active digging had stopped at some point before the war. Neither the Iraqi Army nor the Americans had seen much strategic use for it, and it had been spared destruction from military action. However, free-enterprising Iraqis had allowed coalition forces to visit the area and had opened it up, for lack of a better term, for tourism.

Everyone quickly finished their last bit of food and picked up the trash. I grabbed a couple of waters for the road, drained my bladder one last time, and began to get ready to jump back in the Humvee. Everyone else was doing the same when the lead vehicle took off. The turret gunner jerked backward from the sudden forward acceleration. Gerhard, who was not quite ready, made it to vehicle, jumped in, and started the engine. Brown climbed onto the front bumper, ran up the hood onto the roof, and hopped in the turret. "I'm in!" he shouted.

As the vehicle started to move forward, Oz and I jumped in and pulled the doors shut. Gerhard began yelling, "*Yalla, Yalla*," which was Iraqi for "hurry, hurry" and started to speed up.

"Yeah, yeah, keep your pants on," I said, as I threw my helmet and vest in the seat, trying to hold the door shut until I could get it latched.

We moved up to the weapons clearing area, and again everyone jumped out, and the familiar sound of clacking metal on metal charged the air. Once again, we were reminded that we were in a war. Our mental switch was flipped back on and each soldier placed a full magazine into his weapon, charged it, placed the fire selection lever on safe, and climbed back into the Humvee. The acceleration yanked the vehicle, and we were moving again. Oz turned around and asked, "How long do you think we have?"

"I don't know, give a half hour to forty-five minutes at Ur, and I'm guessing about three more hours or so left on the road," I said. "You gonna call the wife when you get settled down tonight?" I asked.

"Oh yeah, have to; she'll go nuts if I don't," he explained, as I nodded in agreement.

"Yeah, me too. Nadaleane will go crazy if she doesn't hear from me, especially when we're this close to coming home. I should give my mom and dad a call too, but we'll see," I said expressing a little guilt that I hadn't called them more often. We both felt like we had some type of unwritten moral duty to keep our families informed as much as possible. The deployment was hard on them, and all they wanted in return was the regular phone call or a letter that told them we were okay.

Oz gave me that silent look as though he understood how hard it had become to be away for this long of a stretch. Gerhard, listening in, blurted out, "You guys make me sick. Oh, what the hell. Maybe I'll call someone, too, maybe my wife."

Tired of talking, with a full belly, and back inside the warm vehicle, I said, "I'm going to take a little cat nap. Wake me when we get there." As a play on my words both Oz and Gerhard begin purring and whining, imitating kittens. "You're an ass, Gerhard, you too, Oz. Leave me the hell alone, and let me get some sleep" I said and pulled my cap over my eyes, slouching down into the seat and ignoring their banter.

The familiar song of the large Humvee tires on the road and the whine of the engine were again hypnotic. We were as comfortable as we could be and had settled in for the rest of the trip. Hardly a word was spoken as Gerhard maintained his speed and drove to our next stop.

Gradually drifting into that twilight zone where I was not quite asleep but not quite awake either. I occasionally felt Brown as he spun in the turret to his three o'clock position and then, within a few seconds, spun to his nine o'clock position. A few seconds later, he would move back to his twelve o'clock position. The rear gun truck covered the six o'clock position, and the convoy made its way south without incident. Each mile behind us was a mile closer to completing the mission and a day closer to seeing our families again. Although we were still proud to be serving as we did, and as much on the front line that existed, we had long gotten over some of the initial eagerness of going off to war and fighting for God, country and glory. At this point we were just looking out for each other.

Mortars

I CLOSED MY EYES AND tried to position my body in the most comfortable configuration possible to grab a little rest, even a little sleep, but at the very least, try to relax for the remainder of the trip. Soon my mind began to catalog the events of the past year. Maybe the way a librarian sorts through books and places them on the shelves according to the subject matter. Regardless, I had no Dewey Decimal System for all of the events that had taken place. What dominated my memories and thoughts at moments like this, was the 3% chaos I spoke of at the start of this story.

On the ride this day, almost instantly, my thoughts streamed through the mortar attacks of April 2004 and the events in August, November, and many other times during the year when Americans and Iraqi alike had died. My subconscious had done this before and sometimes the events all seemed to blur together and yet remain distinct. I just couldn't quite make sense of everything at once. I kept going over the details of the many mortar attacks. The first major attack to hit the Ganci compound was on April 6, 2004, while I was working in Ganci 2. I was sitting in the CP tent for the camp, having what anyone would call a normal conversation with Sgt. Snyder when . . . Wham!

The first round slammed into the compound. A 120mm mortar round had exploded, sending chunks of hot metal and gravel in all directions and tearing into human flesh, shattering bone, and sending several detainees to the ground. A column of thick, wispy, black smoke shot up, leaving a signature of the impact location. The explosion jarred my whole body from my neck to my ankles. The cordite, the smell of gunpowder, and dust overtook my senses, and my mouth instantly went dry. My heart began to race with adrenaline before my mind could actually process what had happened.

Sgt. Snyder and I both stared at each other for a second and then . . . Wham! Another round hit and sounded even closer than the first. Sgt. Snyder looked at me and yelled, "Mortars!" The second 120mm mortar round landed in what appeared to be Ganci 4, and shrapnel ripped into several detainees inside the compound. A piece of metal approximately the size of a man's thumb penetrated the rear of one man's skull and exited through his right temple, dragging with it sections of reddish and yellowish brain matter. Around the fallen man's head, blood and tissue puddled as he took his last breath. His final exhalations caused the pooling blood to gurgle and bubble on the ground.

We both threw on our helmets as Sgt. Snyder grabbed the radio to call in the attack. I stepped outside the tent and looked toward the other end of the compound when . . . Wham! Another round slammed into Ganci 4, coming dangerously close to the CP tent! We had sand-bagged all four sides of the CPs up to about chest level, and most of the shrapnel was absorbed in that protection. However, I knew if the CP caught a direct hit, the exploding round would more than likely kill everyone inside.

I yelled toward Sgt. Snyder, "Stand fast here," and grabbed my weapon and my combat lifesaver bag and headed out onto the dirt road we called Main Street in the direction of Ganci 4. As I was scrambling out I saw Sergeant 1st Class Breyers, our platoon sergeant, running out as well. "I'm heading to 4. I think they've been hit," I shouted

Sgt. Breyers yelled back, "I'm right behind you," and we both headed towards Ganci 4, which was about 125 to 150 meters away. We were both loaded down with gear like garbage trucks, and with a dry mouth, I got winded quickly.

Usually the Haji's would fire the first few rounds to judge the range of the targets, and within seconds, adjustments were made, and then the full barrage would begin firing for effect.

I was about halfway into the run and caught in the open as the full barrage began to hit. Wham! Wham! Wham! The explosions permeated my ears and drowned out all other audible sounds. Instantly, I took a knee to catch my breath and assess what was going on around me . . . Boom! Rapidly, I dropped to the ground and lay flat, as another round landed close to me. For some unknown reason, I remember looking at my watch and thinking, nice watch. It made no logical sense, but with my arm outstretched, it was the first thing that came to mind.

Another round had hit near the water tower in Ganci 4 and peppered the tower with holes that began to send water raining out onto the powdery, dusty ground. Yet another round slammed near a two-and-a-half ton truck, penetrated its body with shrapnel, and flattened several tires. More rounds slammed into the camp itself and killed at least four detainees, who were taking cover behind a concrete shower structure. Lying on the ground for a moment, I was unaware whether Sgt. Breyers was doing the same thing or had kept going. I raised my head in time to hear two more rounds explode nearby and more rounds continued to pour into the Ganci compound. I thought, *anyplace but here!* I raised myself to my feet and simultaneously leaned into a run. The camps had accelerated into near riotous crowds as men ran for cover and cried out in anger and for help. I pulled my weapon in close preparing to respond to the "whatever" that was going to happen next.

I reached Ganci 4 within a few seconds. Sergeant Breyers ran in next to me and was barely winded. Together, we were standing outside the CP tent at Ganci 4, next to Staff Sergeant Kirk, who was fully and aggressively engaged with trying to manage the turmoil.

Outside in the open, yelling at the top of his lungs Sgt. Kirk was attempting to control what appeared to be madness unfolding inside the camp. Sgt. Kirk turned around to see the both of us standing there, and almost with surprise, he shouted an expletive and asked in his naturally loud voice, "What the hell are you doing here?"

"We thought you took a hit," I said, as another round slammed into a Compound . . . Wham!

"Not yet . . . Get in the bunker!"

Sgt. Breyers and I looked at the small bunker made out of sandbags and Hesco Barriers filled with dirt, to see several men already packed at the door. There was no way we were getting in there. There could have been plenty of room, but we were both a little claustrophobic. I could just see a round hitting the roof of that thing and me being buried alive under all those sandbags. It was not exactly the way I wanted to die.

Specialist Smith was in the doorway of the bunker yelling into the microphone of the radio, "Shadow Main, Shadow Main, Ganci 4 is taking major casualties, heavy concentration of fire, how copy, over? Shadow Main, Shadow Main . . . we need all available medics, how copy?"

Shadow Main was the call sign for the operations center at Abu Ghraib and the nerve center for detainee operations. It was located about a quarter mile in a straight line distance from the Ganci Compound, but walking distance could add another hundred meters.

"Roger, Ganci 4. All medics and MPs are standing fast until the attack is over, Copy Ganci 4?"

At the same time that the shells were exploding inside the camps, the Marines positioned in the outer towers appeared to have located the attacking mortar positions, and the sound of machine guns indicated some attempt to return fire. More than likely, the Hajis were out of range since the mortar barrage continued for several minutes. The sound of mortars exploding, automatic weapons firing, the rapid thump, thump, thump of the MK-19 and the wail of men screaming created chaos on the ear drums. A person could only hear what was being shouted directly to them and the rest became a blur of white noise.

The other camps within the compound were trying to relay similar messages and several rounds had hit the concrete roof of CSH where Gerhard was working. Ganci 6, which was in line with Ganci 4, had also taken direct hits inside the camp and sustained a high number of causalities. The medics and anyone not already caught in the gristmill were ordered to take cover and stand fast until the attack was over. We could not help anyone if we were also wounded, and an ambulance couldn't carry anyone if it was blown-up.

As the mortar barrage continued, dozens of detainees were bringing their wounded and mangled to the gate. Dozens more of near riotous prisoners were gathering en masse screaming for us to help the wounded. Sgt. Kirk was yelling for them to move back. Opening the gate and allowing an overwhelming number of prisoners outside the wire in such chaos could have been disastrous for the soldiers.

"Move back so we can open the gate!" Sgt. Kirk yelled. "When everybody backs away, we'll open the gate!" Sgt. Kirk continued to scream at them, using an Arabic phase we had learned. "*Arg'a! Arg'a!* Move back; move away from the gate." He knew every second wasted was a second that could be used to save someone's life.

Slowly the prisoners understood the order and began to back away from the gate, leaving the wounded, bleeding, and dying. As prisoners began to disperse and take cover, Sgt. Kirk immediately unlocked the gate while several of the camp leaders started hauling out what seemed like an endless line of men with torn flesh and blood soaked clothes.

The first detainee brought out was one of the men that I believed I saw near the concrete showers as I was running toward Ganci 4. He was conscious, but fading fast. He was placed down on the gravel next to the CP tent, just outside the gate. His friend, who had come out with him, was allowed to try to help save his life. The injured detainee wore a white shirt, the back of which was soaked with blood. I knelt and began to do the best I could to access his wounds and save my enemy's life. Together, his friend and I sat the barely conscious man upright. He had several large holes in his back from shrapnel, and he was bleeding heavily. The blood did not seem to coagulate as I expected it to and it was watery. I can still see this man's face. He was in his late forties with grayish hair and a mustache. His friend continued to scream out for me to please try to help him as he held the hand of his severely wounded friend. At that point he wasn't a detainee or a prisoner, he was a man.

With the attack still under way, it will be at least ten or twelve minutes before the medics from the aid station would arrive. I soon realized that I am the only one on the ground in the immediate area with any type of medical bag. *A little more than a Band-Aid* I thought, and began to inventory, in my head, what I thought I was going to be able to do.

Wham! Another round slams into Ganci 6.

Someone shouts, "Let's get some people to 6. They're taking hits, too," and several soldiers blur past me on the run and under fire.

I open my combat lifesaver bag and pull out several field dressings. Seconds seem like minutes and minutes were turning into hours in my mind. Tearing open the green plastic wrapper with my teeth, I pull out the bandage and unravel the tails, surprised to find them dry-rotted from time. I just tore the tails off, and with the aid of his friend, we sat the wounded man up again. I was able to lift his shirt high enough to see and feel the gaping wounds.

"Up a little further," I instructed and signaled with a nodding motion of my head. Now I could see the flow of blood and ragged, torn flesh.

I grab the field dressing, place it over the wound, and tried to apply some duct tape to hold it in place. His back is soaking wet from blood, and the tape will not stick. I stuff the dressing into the open wound, but the white cloth rapidly turns red. It doesn't stop the flow of blood. We repeat this for two additional wounds that left deep holes in the man's back.

I lay him down and watch him open and close his eyes several times as I prepare an IV of saline solution. Holding a catheter in one hand, I begin to tap on his arm in the area where a vein should pop up to provide an easy point to insert the catheter. I slap the area again and wait for the familiar pulse to appear. I see nothing. I lay the line across my leg, grab his arm with both hands, and feel for a spongy area right inside the elbow that signals a flow of blood. Again, nothing.

"Damn it, where are you?" my mind screams. I looked back over my shoulder at Sgt. Breyers, who could see how hard I was trying to save this life, and I could see in his eyes a signal to move on. The man was dead. He probably had a family somewhere and eventually they would mourn his death. There weren't going to be anymore birthdays, he would never hug his children again and whatever was the sum total of his life, it was over now.

I look at the Iraqi man again, and his eyes were not quite open and not quite closed. He had died right there in my hands.

Without hesitating, I shift my position and insert the IV catheter into the arm of another wounded prisoner on my right. He appears to have a large, open wound on his lower abdomen. I handed him a large bandage and tell him to hold it against his bleeding side.

In just a few minutes, there are at least fifteen to twenty wounded prisoners lying on the ground within a few square yards, and the mortar barrage appears to cease. Half of the soldiers in the area are administering first aid with anything available. Soldiers pull out their own field dressing packets, issued for their own use, in an attempt to stop as much bleeding as possible. At one point, I watched a soldier grab a roll of toilet paper and cut it in half with a pair of bandage scissors. With the confidence of an emergency room physician, he stuffed it into the open flesh of a man's shoulder. The wounds are as big as tennis balls, but irregular in shape, and pouring blood. The same soldier then pulls off a large strip of duct tape, slaps it over the wound, and moves on to the next casualty. The remaining soldiers have their hands full keeping the camp under control on what was shaping up to be a full-scale riot. Every soldier learns in basic training how to administer first aid and apply a field dressing. The training is continuously reinforced during a soldier's career, but few truly believe that they would ever actually face anything on the scale of what was unfolding on the battlefield at that moment.

I moved on to another prisoner with a femoral artery bleed as he is trying to apply pressure to his leg with one hand and apply a tourniquet with the other. At the same time I start helping that detainee, another soldier is asking if I have any extra field dressings and if I could set up another IV kit. Immediately, I reached into my Combat Lifesaver Bag, pulled out another field dressing, and toss it to the soldier. Without looking, I pull out another IV bag with tubing and tear open the wrapping of the bag of fluid. Instantly, I pulled the tubing package apart, extend the line and insert the beveled, sharpened edge into the bottom of the bag of clear fluid. I bundle the bag and tubing together, lean over the dead body of my first casualty and hand the IV set to the soldier. I immediately go back to work tightening the tourniquet on the leg of the detainee who is severely bleeding internally; I can see a bulge forming on his inner thigh.

Behind me, Sgt. Breyers is trying to help Sgt. Kirk control the gate and maintain security while the madness continues to escalate. As the wounded are pulled out of Ganci 4, Sgt. Breyers attempts to organize some triage.

"Let's move the dead to one side and treat the wounded right here as they come out!" Sgt. Breyers commands the soldiers helping with the wounded.

"How many more wounded? I ask. "I'm running out of supplies here. Anyone not hurt needs to get out of here!"

A solid fifteen minutes passes since the first round had hit the compound, but it seems like an hour. I briefly looked down Main Street for a second and can see several combat ambulances heading in our direction with a two-and-a-half ton truck directly behind. I thank God they are here. My medical bag is depleted, and we have scores more wounded. The combat ambulances roll up, and the Army Medics and Navy corpsmen jump out and get to work.

"Man, am I glad to see you guys . . . I'm out of everything," I say.

The medics ask me, "What do we have going on here?"

"Femoral artery bleed on this one, internal femoral artery bleed again here . . . I think the round hit him in the leg and didn't explode. Shrapnel to the abdominal on this guy," I explain as I point to each one.

"I could use some more field dressings, if you have them."

"Roger that." And the Navy Corpsman hands me a handful of green packets.

I told him that some would be ready as soon as they could get them loaded. My adrenaline was still pumping hard, but with numerous other medics and corpsman now on site, I started to help load the wounded on the back of the truck for the trip to the combat support hospital on the FOB, where Gerhard was managing his own level of chaos. We packed as many as we could into the bed of a 2 ½ ton truck. A couple of hard slaps on the door to signal the driver, and the truck pulled off. Right in line, another one rolled up waiting to be loaded.

The next truck stops, and from the driver's seat jumps our very own Command Sergeant Major Vacho. There wasn't much time for conversation, but I could see in his face he was stunned at the number of wounded. Again, we loaded as many as would fit into the bed of the truck. Sgt. Maj. Vacho helped with the loading and then climbed back into the cab, released the parking brake and looked over his shoulder to me.

Someone asked, "What about this one?" He was standing near the first detainee that I had worked on at the beginning of the attack, the one that had died in my hands. He was now a detainee again. I had to remove the emotion from the moment and get back on the job. I had to take what I felt about the situation off the table and do what I was trained to do; I had to be a soldier.

"No," I replied. "He's dead." I gave the sergeant major a thumbs up in the mirror and slapped the back of the truck bed. He put the truck into gear and eased off the clutch. As the truck lurched forward a little and began to move, a waterfall of blood and fluid flowed from the truck bed and down the tailgate. I could not help but stare at that one image for a moment. That tragically symbolic picture froze time for a second as I thought about the litter of a battlefield. Briefly, I again looked at the face of the dead detainee who had left this life from my arms. Others had died, and more would die in the future, but he had been the first I could not save. I did not see the exact moment that this man sustained his wounds, but I was sure I was in the general area when the round that eventually killed him exploded. It was hard not to think about my own mortality and ask myself why him and not me. At one point or another every soldier who goes into combat considers how random the selection becomes during the course of a battle and wonders, *how did I make it out of that one?*

During this time, Spc. White was at Ganci 6 dealing with much of the same around him. A detainee elder, a camp chief, had been severely hit, losing part of one leg and one arm. Additionally, shrapnel had torn a large portion of his skull open, penetrating the roof of his mouth. Unbelievably, the man was still alive, at least for a few moments. Spc. White held the prisoner's head as he tried to speak his final words. His mouth opened and his lips moved, and portions of brain matter dribbled down the corners of his mouth. The more he tried to speak, the more his mouth would fill with his own brain matter and blood until he just did not try anymore. White and I briefly spoke about this event one time, several days after the attack. We both just looked at each other in silence for a few moments. We never talked about it again.

Thirty Minutes as a Tourist

Bang, bang, bang. "Wake up down there," Brown yelled down through the turret. Slowly, my eyes found the daylight again. Never fully asleep and never completely awake either, I must have gone down well enough to get about forty-five minutes to an hour of a semi-restful snooze, in spite of the vehicle. Military vehicles were usually built for the mission, and your size, comfort, or discomfort was not always a priority.

Bang, bang. "Are you up, Wass?" Brown slapped the roof of the vehicle again.

"Yeah, Yeah," I said and waved my hand to let him know I was awake as he poked his head down into the hole, while peeking through his desert scarf.

"What's up?" Oz asked, enthralled with one of his puzzle books. I gave him a tug on the back of his shoulder.

"I think we're at Ur," I said and began to sit up more alertly.

"Wow, that was quick. Are you all rested now, Sleeping Ugly?" Oz asked.

"Screw you," I said and repositioned my body back up into the seat.

Off in the distance, we could see the structured shape of a manmade mountain on a mountain. I noticed signs of an airfield to my right, most certainly an American or British airfield now. The evidence of American soldiers was present as we made our way up a long and easily winding road to this pyramid-like shape. We reached what appeared to be the top of a large hill, and then drove into an open area that seemed to suggest a parking lot, but not really a parking lot.

Again, we went through the routine of dismounting from the vehicles, securing them, and stretching our bodies. Lt. Bodiker called us together in a loose formation and gave us a hasty briefing, including how long we had to do a little sightseeing.

"This is Ur. We have about thirty minutes here, and then we're back on the road," Lt. Bodiker said. "Take pictures, look around, but be back here in thirty minutes. I'll stay with the vehicles."

We began to walk over to the ruins. Brown jumped down from the turret and called out to the rest of us, "Hey, wait up, guys."

It appeared to be an archeological site, but the digging had stopped before the war began in March 2003. Up a gentle slope and at the edge of the parking area, there were several large signs describing the archeological ruins in several languages. The large structure we had seen from afar was known as the Ziggurat of Ur. It was somewhat like the Mayan pyramids, with a long set of steps that led up the center. The top on the structure was flat and perhaps not the full height as originally built.

Brown, Gerhard, Osborne, and I quickly climbed the steps to the top and stood there for a few moments looking out over the vastness of the desert. There was not a lot to see, even from that height, except for earthen bricks and sand. But for just a moment, I think we all felt pretty small on this one large piece of history.

Leave it to Brown to break up the moment. "Hey, Oz, let's get a picture of me, with you looking like you're pushing me over the edge."

"Great idea! Gerhard, you take the picture," Oz said, and Brown gave Gerhard the camera.

I could do nothing but laugh and asked, "What is this, National Lampoon's Iraqi Vacation?" A little more clowning around, a few more pictures, and back down the steps we went. On the way down, we stopped and paired up for some of those "best buddy, I was there" photos. At the bottom again, we split off for a few minutes of individual exploring. I wandered through some of the ruins, mostly stone and earthen walls, the remnants of the foundations of the old city. I could easily see that it was more than just a small group of houses bunched together. The writing on the signs described Ur as the birthplace of Abraham. The Bible and the Torah both tell us a great deal about Abraham and even mentions the city of Ur in the text. It was hard to wrap my mind around the fact that we were walking that very same ground that was written about thousands of years before. Very few people in the world would ever get the chance to set foot here, and even fewer Americans would have this opportunity.

Our thirty minutes were almost up, and we began to make our way back to the vehicles. As we walked, we noticed a small trailer with the sides opened up similar to that of a street-side hot-dog vendor. The trailer, out of place in the desert and certainly out of character for a war zone, was a souvenir stand. In the front sat an elderly Iraqi gentleman selling trinkets and souvenirs to anyone visiting the historic site. Oz, surprised at the capitalistic nature commented, "Look at this, all we need now is a group of Japanese tourists with cameras around their necks."

Oz cracked me up sometimes with what I thought were hilariously unsuitable comments that rolled out of his mouth. Out of all this madness, death, and destruction sat an old man just trying to make a buck. "Oz, come on, let's buy something," I said.

"I'm not buying anything from here. I don't want to remember this place."

"Yeah, you do. Come on," I continued to prod him.

Together we walked over to the old man and looked at his wares. For a guy with a trailer in the desert, he had a good selection of items from which to choose. We laid down ten dollars and bought a small, ceramic plaque with a pressed paper wood backing. The image in the ceramic was that of the ziggurat, the very mountain of steps we had just climbed. As the years have begun to tick by, the small plaque that Oz did not want to buy, from a place he did not want to remember, has become highly valued and hangs in his home today.

Randomly, we began to collect ourselves back at the vehicles and prepared to get back on the road. Again, in an almost somber motion, we each checked our gear, charged our weapons, and mounted our Humvees for another couple of hours driving. The seriousness returned to our faces as we ended our visit as tourists.

The squelch broke on the radio, "Shadow Move to Shadow units. Be advised we will be pulling out in two mikes. Shadow Guard, Shadow Trail how copy?"

"Shadow Guard, we're guns up," Oz replied.

"Shadow Trail, we're guns up," an anonymous voice replied.

Within minutes, the lead vehicle's large rear tires yanked the rear of the vehicle's body downward, and the sudden movement jerked the gunner. The Humvee had begun to build a little speed down the dusty dirt road, and our Humvee followed. Shadow Trail kicked up a cloud of dust as well as they fell in behind and tried to catch up with our vehicle before we hit the main road. In our mirrors, we said goodbye to the brief vacation and the birthplace of the first patriarch of the Old Testament. Now, all we would have to remember this moment were a few photos, cheap souvenirs, and our forever-fading memories.

All of us expected to be home by early spring. In the big picture, our little stopover at Ur probably would not register in our recollections as a great event. Although a theologian would more than likely find the location and the biblical history awe-inspiring. An archeologist would most certainly believe that the ruins were worth limitless time investigating. To me, as a soldier in a war, it was just another place. I am sure the breathtaking view at the top of the ziggurat captured a solemn moment in everyone's mind, but it was only a moment.

Our small convoy wound its way back down the road, retracing the same narrow path back onto the main supply route towards Camp Bucca in southern Iraq. It was about 1400 hours and we expected to roll through the gate within about two hours. For now, no one was sleepy, just bored. We were impatient with the long ride and were antsy with the constant sitting.

The Humvee rode and drove fairly well on the open road, but in time, it was a little hard on the human body. However, Humvees were a great improvement over the M-151 Jeep the Army used until the early 1980s. The Humvees were more spacious than the old jeeps, but they were still tight considering all of the equipment that modern soldiers had to carry. No one had any real leg room, and it was difficult, if not impossible, to fire your weapon out the window. The rear of the Humvee contained a lot of little equipment holders and tie downs that, most of the time, were not used and seemed to just be something to snag your gear on when pulling it out.

To their credit, Humvees are fast. Over smooth road, they can reach an average speed of about sixty miles per hour without straining, and they usually set the pace for the convoys in Iraq, although we could not go any faster than the slowest vehicle and still maintain the unity of the convoy. The driver had a good cockpit setup. Everything was within arm's reach. The hand brake, lights, and gauges were all military standard. The gunner had the best seat of all. He could see 360 degrees and could stand or rig a seat with a sling in the gunner's hatch. The vehicle was also very adaptable and was designed to accommodate a variety of weapons configurations. Soldiers could mount a machine gun, a TOW anti-tank missile system, or the MK 19 grenade launcher, along with various radio configurations. Overall, they were rugged and could take a lot of punishment. I know we nearly drove the wheels off of them, and with a moderate amount of maintenance, they kept on running.

In what seemed like no time at all, one and a half or two hours had passed, and Camp Bucca came into sight. Several miles away, on the horizon, we could see small outlines of tents and trailers. In another area on the horizon was the silver shimmer of fencing of the prison compound. I gave a yank on Brown's pants leg again to get his attention.

Brown gave the top of the Humvee a tap, and we heard him say, "I see it. We're here." The vertical shapes of the guard towers and the tall floodlights were visible and waiting for sunset to silhouette them against the desert.

We followed the lead vehicle to a main gate area and stopped at the weapons clearing barrel. Again, I heard the familiar sounds of charging handles being pulled to the rear and the ejected rounds hitting the sand and still more clicking with the removal of the magazines. We bent down to pick up our ejected rounds and pressed them back into the magazines, just as we had done a thousand times before. Without thinking and without looking, we stuffed the magazines into pouches on our vests and climbed back into our vehicles. Each of us held our weapons as familiar friends. We closed the dust covers on the sides of the weapons, wiped the outer surfaces with small rags, and, instantly, our thumbs rubbed over the fire selector switches on the left side of the weapon, ensuring that they were on safe. The lead vehicle kicked a small cloud of dust from the tires and moved off in the direction of a group of sleeping trailers. Our three vehicles rolled into a gravel parking lot and pulled side by side. We had made it to our destination and we were now on our time. I heard the squeaking of the heavy metal hinges as the up-armored doors opened and soldiers began to unload. For the next twelve hours, this was going to be home.

Spc. Gillman and Lt. Bodiker, who had made this trip a few times before, walked over and said, "You guys hold up here for a few moments. We'll check in and find our building."

"No problem," I said as I began taking my body armor off. Gillman, the Lieutenant, and the rest of what we called "the inside group" walked off to square away the business of the mission. Spc. Gillman needed to check in with the person managing the transient billeting. Each FOB usually had a place where soldiers, as well as civilians could spend the night if they were either coming or going to another FOB or were held over for some unknown reason. Some locations that have seen more traffic than others may have had a little more luxury associated with the accommodations, and usually an NCO was assigned to manage the assets.

Lazily, Brown, Gerhard, Osborne, and I just sat back on the hood of the vehicles and admired the setting sun as it slowly fell from the sky and gave way to twilight and floodlights. It was hard to believe it was actually peaceful. If there was any beauty in this place, it was in the sunsets. The orange, yellow, and red hues would fan out as they hit the desert and treat your eyes with a sensational display before disappearing below the horizon. We looked around, and began to see things at Bucca that were foreign to us as they related to Iraq and specifically anywhere near Abu Ghraib.

At first, we noticed everyone was walking around wearing soft caps and without their Individual Body Armor (IBA). Who were these aliens to the war zone? Located between two large air supported structures were volleyball courts. They had outside leisure activities in Iraq? This was not in our world back at Abu. We soon noticed that those few moments that Gillman said he would be gone had turned into half an hour. It became apparent that we had been forgotten that we were waiting. As close as soldiers can be, they also divide into their cliques. It was obvious that we were not part of the inside team. Another fifteen minutes passed before Spc. Gillman walked up and asked, "What are you guys waiting for?"

Gerhard fired back, "You! Where have you been?"

The embarrassment on Gillman's face told us that he had forgotten about coming back and showing us where the billeting was located. Brown yanked up his gear and calmed the situation with, "No harm, No foul. Let's dump this gear and get something to eat." We grabbed our rucks, threw them over our shoulders, and followed Gillman to a large doublewide trailer among a line of trailers that had been set up as sleeping quarters.

"Grab a bunk anywhere. The females are in this corner," Spc. Gillman explained.

We moved to the far corner opposite another entrance door. Oz and Gerhard threw their packs on a bunk and flopped down as if they were at home, in their living room. Already, I could see that an outdoor light was going to shine through a door window and blind me all night.

I grabbed a mattress, pulled it down onto the floor, and moved into a corner in a vain effort to hide from a flood light hoisted high just outside the door. Throughout the deployment all of us had our sleep patterns disrupted, and I felt I couldn't get to sleep at all some nights. Oz would tell me that he didn't think I would be able to get to sleep unless I was in the back of a Chinook helicopter. The Chinook had long cargo nets for seats that felt like a hammock when I would lay down in them. I would put my earplugs in and let the helicopter rock me to sleep. Many times we would not get word that we were going to leave on a mission until late in the afternoon, after we had already worked a full day either in the Ganci compound or the IHA. At that point, we were naturally tired and the little rest we were able to get on a helicopter was possibly what would have to carry us through until the mission was completed.

Eventually I had my little corner arranged and laid down for a minute just to see if it would be comfortable. No sooner had I closed my eyes, than Gerhard kicked me in the foot and said, "Get up, Wassmonster. Let's go get something to eat." I had maybe fifteen minutes of rest and although a little hungry, I was not ready to get up just yet.

"Is Oz ready?" I asked.

"He's over there folding his undies," Gerhard replied with a smirk.

With a groan and a moan, I stood up and grabbed my weapon, and we headed out the door.

Looking over the sprawling camp, I asked, "Does anyone have a clue where the chow hall is located?" Without speaking Gerhard slapped his pants leg, pulled out his cap, and put it on his head without breaking stride.

Oz said, "Yeah, just look for a line of guys throwing up."

In an optimistic tone, I respond, "It's not that bad. We've had some good food every now and again."

"Yeah, really?" Oz replied. "This is the guy who was on his knees, puking up crab legs." He was referring to an incident when I had undoubtedly contracted some sort of food poisoning through seafood that was served to us back at Abu.

Less than a hundred yards out our door, we found what the Army calls the DFAC or dining facility. The line was not long, and we shuttled through the usual fare of fried fast foods or the more steak-and-potatoes, home-cooked style. Again, we sat down to another fine meal prepared for us by the U.S. Government. We scattered our dinner with some light conversation until Oz asked one of those foreboding questions, "Wass, do you remember when Gillman told us when Gasiewicz got killed?"

"Yeah, we were kind of sitting at the table for chow just like this," I said. Then I asked, "Do you remember when Doc got killed?"

"Yeah," Oz said in a quiet voice.

I continued, "I had just rolled into the field hospital that day with the detainee that got hit in the leg, and you could hear the bullets hitting the concrete walls all over the place. There on the table in the E.R. was Doc."

"I remember that. What a crazy day that was," replied Oz.

"I remember Doc's straw cowboy hat," Gerhard said somberly.

I asked Gerhard and Oz, "You guys saw it when Major Steeple loaded those four Marines that were killed from an IED attack in April of last year, right?" Oz and Gerhard both nodded their heads in solemn acknowledgement, and surely, they felt that words were not necessary.

Most of us remembered the Marines because we were listening to the radio chatter that particular evening and heard when they called for support. We heard them ask for the medevac and listened as a firefight seemed to delay the help coming to their aid. The next morning we heard that four Marines had been killed. Oz, Gerhard, and many other soldiers watched as four body bags were loaded on a truck, for the eventual return to their families. The Sgt. Major and the rest of us knew about their sacrifice before four mothers knew their sons were dead. The feeling of those events stuck with everyone for a while. We all knew that we were in an ugly place, doing an ugly business, but every once in a while a moment got branded into our minds that reminded us that we were not dreaming and that this war had a real cost.

Anne Gasiewicz and Jeff Serrette (Doc) had been killed during the year, and both deaths had hit me harder than I had expected. I did not know either of them well, but I had worked with or around them briefly at different times. Mostly, we would see each other in the chow hall or at the phone bank. And often, while waiting for the phone or the Internet, we did what soldiers do and struck up a conversation, and for those few moments, they were my friends.

At this point, we were just sitting there staring at our food, not actually saying anything, nodding our heads and playing with the utensils. Each of us was lost in our thoughts for a second and thinking of the events more intensely than we had done before.

I finally broke the silence and stood up. "Let's get out of here," I said. "I have to call the wife and check my e-mail." Oz and Gerhard stood up, and we headed to the exit and dumped our trays in the trash cans just outside the door. With a familiar slap to the pants leg, we pulled out our hats from the cargo pocket and put them on before we had walked more than three steps.

Gerhard yelled out, "Hooah!" and told us, "I'll see you guys later." We gave him a fist pound as he headed out in search of some Gerhard-style adventure. He could take care of himself, but this could be anything from working out at the gym to telling lies to an army nurse.

Oz slapped me on the back and said, "Let's go see what our better halves are doing."

"Yeah, let's do that. I told her we were headed out on a convoy, and she was not happy."

We looked around and saw what looked like a gym or social area and Internet café. Sure enough, we walked into a large prefabricated building and found the phones, internet, TV, gym, and game rooms. Once again, we were amazed and looked at each other as if we had just landed on another planet. We were starting to get a few luxuries back at Abu, but nothing like the scale of what we were seeing at Bucca. I guessed we should not complain. If they had it, they should flaunt it. And at that moment, we used it and enjoyed it.

The usual procedure was to get into a line and wait. As phones became available, the line moved forward. Sometimes, when I didn't use the sat-phone, I waited as long as forty-five minutes or maybe longer, and then I would have to do the same routine for the computer. On this day, however, the line was short and there was a large phone bank set up. Within a few minutes, two phones became available. Oz and I jumped down into the semi-private space of the booth and started dialing our wives. There is an eight-hour time difference between Iraq and the East Coast of the United States. This translated into a four- to six-second delay in the communication. It was a little awkward at first. We would say something and wait to hear the other person speak. Before they could hear our voices, they were asking, "Hello, Hello?" Then they heard us and started talking. Before we heard their voice back, we would try to explain the delay, and it ended up sounding like an Abbott and Costello comedy bit. It took a little while until everyone got the hang of it.

Our families waited patiently near the phone on specific days and at specific times just to speak with us a few minutes and for us to reassure them that everything was okay. We were usually busy and may not have actually wanted to make the calls home, but we considered that our families often waited nervously for those few minutes to hear our voices. On a regular basis at Abu, and sometimes at other forward operating bases, we would come under attack during the phone conversations. Our family members could hear loud explosions in the background as we talked, and on a few occasions, we felt it was necessary to get off the phone quickly. Most of the time, however, we would keep talking, but had a little white lie prepared to explain the loud noises in the background. In my case, I claimed the noise was from the trash truck. My wife or mom would be reassured that I was not in any danger and, therefore, did not stay awake worrying all night.

After a few rings, my wife picked up and I said hello and waited.

I heard, "Hello," and then "Sweetie pie!" squealed out from the other end.

"Yes, baby, it's me," I said.

"I love you, Sweetheart . . . I miss you dearly. When are you coming home, baby?" Nadaleane asked. She would always ask and I would always say, "Soon."

"I don't exactly know, but soon," I told her.

Nadaleane was upset when I was deployed. We had been married barely a year when I got called two days before her birthday. She would tell anyone that every day I was gone was miserable for her. I had met her while on another deployment to Germany, and we had married two years later. Nadaleane was originally from Egypt and understood the cruelty that could exist in the Middle East. Profoundly religious and Christian, she prayed for my buddies and for me every day and often sent out mass e-mails to many of her friends to do the same when she felt nervous about something relating to me.

Quickly, we became engaged in our usual conversation. We traded the soft "I love you" and then got caught up on each other's latest and greatest news of the day. I asked about my son and my parents and about how work was going for her. It didn't take long before there was nothing left to talk about, and I was tired.

"Gerit, can you come home early, sweetheart?" Nadaleane asked me as she had asked before. "I miss you so much."

"You know I can't do that. This is not summer camp or a bad vacation," I replied.

Nadaleane, almost in tears, "I just miss you baby, I need you near me."

"I understand, sweetie pie, but let me get this thing done and we'll be able to spend plenty of time together," I tried to comfort her longing and desperation in my absence. It tore me apart having to say no to her pleas, but there was little choice for me.

"Baby, I really need to go. I'm falling fast, and I need to get to bed. We have a long drive tomorrow," I said, understanding her need to know that I was okay. "I am good and I'll be home before you know it."

"Okay, sweetie pie, I love you. Please call me tomorrow if you can, I need to hear your voice," she said before she hung up the phone.

I could hear Oz getting off the phone about the same time when Gerhard walked up. He had just checked his e-mail and was heading back to the trailer.

"You guys heading back, too?" Gerhard asked.

"Yeah, we're beat," Oz replied and asked "How is Nadaleane, Wass?"

I replied with some hesitation, "She is hanging in there, but some days it seems like it is only by a finger nail. She misses me, she wants me home and I think she is just getting worn thin."

Oz understood, "I know, Harriett too, she hates that I am gone and I miss my son."

"What do we do guys?" I asked. "We're torn between home and duty."

Oz replied, "We just keep doing it until it ends."

Together, the three of us shuffled back through the soft sand to our bunks. By now, the floodlights had come on all over camp, and what nightlife you can have in Iraq came alive from everyone who was not an MP. We were drained, ready for a hot shower and a good night's sleep, which made all the difference in the world when we could get it.

From Seventeen to Forty-Two

EVERYONE EXCEPT OSBORNE SPENT A restless night of tossing and turning in bed until Lt. Bodiker kicked us loose around 0530. That is two hours past zero-dark-thirty, so we actually slept in a bit. I spent most of the night lying awake, thinking if I got to sleep right at that moment, I would get four hours of rest or three and a half hours of rest. I did not get to sleep until sometime around 0100 hours. When I woke up, I wasn't completely exhausted, but just a little tired. Gerhard nodded off early and had gotten up several times during the night, presumably to go to the bathroom or take a walk. Throughout the night, I could hear bed frames squeak and doors close as different soldiers were getting up and leaving their bunks to go for a smoke, sit outside, or make a run to the latrine. I didn't realize it at the time, but a year at Abu had worn everyone down, and most seemed to have a little trouble sleeping.

Osborne was the one person I knew who could fall asleep, stay asleep, and do nothing but snore. Once he went down, anyone would be hard pressed to wake him up with feeble noises. During the long hours with no days off working in the detention camps, Osborne's squad had set up a cot in the corner of the CP tent, which allowed a soldier to get a short nap, if needed, during the slow parts of a shift. One evening, while Oz was taking his little nap, the compound came under fire from mortars. Osborne's fellow soldiers could not wake him up. Even with the loud explosions hitting nearby, he snored through the attack. One of his team members simply laid his body armor across his chest, put his helmet on, grabbed Oz's weapon, and headed for the bunker. Later they said that if there was nothing left of him when they returned, they would just tell his wife he died in his sleep.

The lights came on inside the trailer. Everyone was getting dressed and packing up for the ride back. Gerhard, Oz, and I cleaned up our bunk area and stowed our gear in a corner until after we ate. We walked over to the chow hall and stood in the usual line for the usual breakfast, which happened to be the best meal of any cooked in Iraq. After all, it's hard to screw up eggs, waffles with hot syrup, or toast with jelly. On the really good days, the smell of smoked sausage links or cooked bacon hung in the air as an invitation to come inside. While we were eating, Lt. Marana came over to our table and gave us a brief situation report. When we were finished, we were to grab our gear and move our Humvee over to the main gate of the prison compound. We would all meet up there then break down into our details.

Lt. Marana also said, "Give your rifles to Gillman, and he will drive them back in his vehicle with Lt. Bodiker and Sgt. Garner."

"Roger that, sir," we replied and gave him a nod as we kept eating.

Gerhard dumped his tray and said, "Grab my gear and meet me at the truck," as he headed out the door and to where we had parked the vehicles the day before.

I looked at Oz and asked, "Are you ready?" And I downed the last swallow of my orange juice as we were getting up.

"Yeah, let's blow this popsicle stand," Oz replied, and we went to grab our packs, stashed back at the trailer

Gillman, Garner, and the other soldiers were all drifting in at regular intervals as others got up and left. Sgt. Brown was still eating, but would be driving the same vehicle back that we rode down in the day before. He was going to meet up with us at the compound and wasn't in as big hurry.

We joined Gerhard and started to unload anything that wasn't necessary for the long return trip. Our packs, extra food, and even my medical bag were going into the back of Gillman's Humvee. Oz attempted to open the back hatch, but the latch was typically stuck. Oz gave it a hard thrust upwards, and a small cloud of dust blasted into the air as the lock broke free and the hatch sprung open. We tossed our gear into the back, put our rifles on top, and slammed the hatch shut. We were down to what we called our battle rattle—shotguns and ammo, some food and water, and our ballistic vests and helmets. Gerhard began the preventive maintenance checks on our Humvee and got her warmed up for the quick drive over to the detention camps.

Gerhard shouted over his shoulder, "Let me know if I have tail lights."

"Yeah," I replied and gave him the international sign for okay, a thumbs-up.

"Signals?" Gerhard asked, as he went through a series of checks.

Walking around to the front, I shouted, "Ready?" We repeated the checks for the headlights.

"It's all good," I said and sat down in the warmth of the truck.

Oz jumped into a back seat, and we drove toward the detention compound, which was easily identified by the tall floodlights, silvery chain link fence that we had seen the day before, and the hundreds of detainees in yellow jumpsuits walking without purpose inside the fence line. The different camps within the compound were divided by dirt roads used as drive isles and were dotted with white guard towers. We pulled our vehicle next to another Humvee and waited. Gerhard left the engine running while other vehicles pulled alongside, and together, we hung around expecting the buses to arrive. Lt. Marana anxiously walked to the compound CP hut to see what the plan of action was for the morning. He, above all people, knew that we needed to get on the road as soon as possible. Delays meant being on the road longer than necessary, most likely after dark.

We tried to absorb the last few ounces of heat from inside the vehicle and sat quietly until we needed to get out and turn the vehicle over to Brown. After a respectable twenty minutes, we broke away from the steel nest and headed down a path in the direction of the camp. Lt. Marana, appearing more angry than calm, met us about halfway and explained the obvious: the buses had not arrived. Supposedly, two buses had been prearranged through the operations section with some of the locals, friendly to Coalition forces, in a type of a contractor arrangement. Dependability of the Hajis was always questionable, and plans constantly fluctuated in response to their availability.

"They're not here. I am going find out what's the hold up," he said to us stomping off in the opposite direction.

He believed there was some type of mix-up. Possibly, they were never scheduled or maybe had the wrong dates. He headed over to the civilian motor park to try and straighten out the situation or at least get two different buses to make the trip back to Abu. We were beginning to believe that the planning part of this trip left a lot to be desired. Our job was not to get too deep into the logistics of the mission, just make sure it was executed properly. We stood by and waited as the issue was worked out. Later on, we considered the fact that this miscommunication played a bigger role for us in the mission.

It was 0730 on January 12, 2005, and the morning air held onto the chill. We pulled out the flight gloves we had stuffed in our cargo pockets and rubbed our hands together swiftly to generate some friction. We liked our flight gloves. They were thick enough to keep our hands warm, but thin enough to allow us to fire our weapons or drive the Humvee. We continued to walk toward the compound and found Spc. Gillman, who helped us locate the NCO in charge of the transfer. Introductions were brief and scattered with small talk as we explained the bus situation. The NCOIC understood, and the Bucca guards had already begun to line the detainees up along the inside of the fence, also waiting.

We lingered in the path between the camps and, in doing so, became aware of some very real differences in the way these camps were constructed as compared to the camps at Abu. First were the guard towers. They appeared to have been professionally built out of metal with a real stair system leading up to the guard hut. The front had a window made from a relatively thick section of Plexiglas, and they had a combination heater and air conditioner inside. It can get cold in Iraq, so this was a big step up from the wooden boxes we had at Abu. Secondly, the guards were not wearing any body armor or Kevlar helmets. Instead, they wore reflective vests and soft caps. We asked ourselves, "Is this the same war?" The detainees also had better than average living quarters, and the unofficial word was they also had good food.

Before the detainees were brought outside the compound, we were told that they had not been searched, and this process was time-consuming, at best. The Bucca MPs told us that they were not sure when we were going to leave, and they did not want to have the prisoners just standing around for an unknown departure time. In any case, it was left up to the escort team to do the body searching and go through all of their belongings. It was not truly a problem. We figured it was all in a day's pay, but we thought that just out of plain curiosity, the other MPs would at least throw in and help us out. Oz counted the yellow jumpsuits lined up against the inside of the fence, and instead of seventeen or eighteen detainees, he counted forty-two.

Oz walked over to the NCOIC of the compound and said, "Sergeant, we were told we had seventeen detainees heading back. I'm counting forty-two."

"Yeah, I know" he replied. "They added a few late yesterday afternoon." Oz, Gerhard, and I just looked at each other for a second, knowing that this was one of those moments when we needed to adapt our plan. Bewildered, we shook our heads, knowing that the one thing that was constant was change. Flexibility was the word of the day.

I asked Oz, "Well, what do you think we should do?"

Oz shook his head, "I don't know, man. How many does one of those buses hold?"

Gerhard spoke up, "It's about forty, give or take a few."

Twenty-four extra bodies would not normally create a problem, but for us, it was how many would fit on a single bus? The original plan was to have two MPs on one bus, and Oz was a last-minute addition. Would the additional bodies divide the three of us onto two buses? Where would the detainee's belongings be stored? It, in essence, reshaped the mission.

Two buses were never going to work well from the beginning when it was just two of us as guards, unless one was planned as storage or backup. Sitting seventeen on one bus had to have been the primary plan. Having twenty-four added bodies was going to pack the bus full from front to rear. Typically, we would have tried to put a few seats between the detainees and us. I looked at Oz and Gerhard and found some agreement in their eyes.

"All three of us together on this trip, right?" I said with some assertion.

Oz replied, "Oh, yeah, but the lieutenant might not like it."

"Screw it, this is what we have to do," Gerhard said. "We'll pack all of their crap on the other bus, put them on one bus, and we take the front two seats."

We agreed, and Oz walked off to find the lieutenant and give him a heads up on the new plan. We figured the lieutenant couldn't care less how we packed them on or specifically who guarded them. What he cared about was getting them all back to Abu and the minor details of how became our problem.

The Bucca MPs began bringing the prisoners out, four at a time. Gerhard and I started the individual searching of each detainee. We each grabbed one while two were held at the ready. After doing hundreds, maybe even a few thousand, of these body searches, we had become quite proficient, and yet it was still our least favorite task to perform. Anyone who worked in law enforcement understood the level of disgusting items that can be found on the human body. We would pull a detainee and have him place his hands against the fence. Starting from the head and working down, we felt through their hair, along the arms and armpits, along each leg and foot, wrapping it up with a feel of the unmentionables and a swipe up the butt crack. Over the course of the year, we had found notes, maps, weapons, and U.S. currency stashed in various forbidding places. Nothing was a surprise anymore.

We began to bark out commands in what could have easily been perceived as loud, angry voices to the casual untrained observer. It could have even appeared that we were mean, violent, and spiteful men who took out our displeasure on the captured enemy. In reality, it was an intimidation and control factor that provided us a valuable edge in managing what was always the numerical disadvantage. In essence, our demeanor and voice gave us authoritative control over the situation and defined without question who was in charge.

During the searching, the Bucca guard working closely with us approached Gerhard and me and said, "We don't really yell at the detainees like that here." Gerhard and I just looked at him for a moment in astonishment. I think we both thought the guy was on drugs or kidding around, but he wasn't. He was serious.

"The command didn't want us screaming at them. I think we have to show a lot more patience and tolerance than you guys do," he explained.

"Yeah, yeah, I guess so." I had to act as though I was not shocked.

Gerhard stood up from searching a prisoner and said, "Well, I guess it's a good thing that they're not going to be here much longer." He then barked out another profane command to a prisoner to move forward and proceeded through with the search.

The young Bucca guard said, "Hey, I know where you guys have been. We heard that you have been taking a beating up there at Abu, and I know you get some real crazies right off the battlefield, but here, they don't want us to ratchet it up unless we have to."

"No problem," I said, accommodating his need to explain. "Hopefully we'll be out of here relatively soon. We're already running late."

Osborne walked back up and I asked him, "Well, what did the lieutenant have to say?"

Osborne said, "The lieutenant doesn't care. He said to just get them on the bus and let's get them back."

"Just as we had thought, our problem," I said.

Oz began helping us search the personal bags that each prisoner had intended to bring back to Abu with him. During a detainee's confinement, he was given certain amenities that made his life a bit more comfortable. Toothpaste, sandals, blankets, and clothing were all common items among a prisoner's belongings. What was forbidden, however, frequently changed, and the detainees stockpiled items, never sure that what was acceptable one day would be acceptable another day. In order to carry all of their stuff, most of the prisoners made handbags out of extra clothes, MRE bags, or anything available that could be sewn together. These handbags were actually quite unique. They showed a great deal of workmanship and were extremely artful. Occasionally, detainees were given a small athletic style bag, but regardless, everyone had something to carry his stuff.

That day, each detainee had two or three of these bags. We decided to limit the number of bags to two per detainee with two blankets. Even with this restriction, it gave us eighty-four bags and eighty-four blankets, which would fill up the rear quarter of a bus. Our decision to place all the bags on one bus and to pack everyone on the other bus was the most logical way to go.

Gerhard and I continued with the searching of the prisoners as Oz went through the bags. Slowly, a pile began to build of items that were not going to leave the camp. The detainees did not have any of the prohibited items with them. Their belongings were more sentimental as opposed to necessary, but they wanted to carry everything regardless. Sentimental was not on our menu at the time, and we knew they would be given more blankets, clothes and sandals again, if they needed them.

Each detainee pleaded in broken English, "Please, mister, one more bag. Please, mister, only these blankets. Please, mister, why this?"

Again, in loud, angry voices we just pointed and told them to move on. In thirty minutes, we were finished with the searching and had the prisoners separated from the camp, ready to board. But where were the buses? It was 0830 and we were at least one hour late getting on the road, and by this time, everyone was beginning to get anxious. A cloud of white vapors formed as the detainees grouped together, blowing on their hands to keep them warm.

Within a few minutes, we could see our rides coming from a distance, in the form of two older red and silver buses. They were being led by a Humvee and headed toward the compound. The main gate was opened, and the buses rolled up to the area where the other vehicles were grouping up and preparing to leave. Gerhard took command of the detainees, got them lined up and ready to board.

"Stand up," he shouted and motioned upward with his hands. "*Erfa! Erfa!*" he shouted. This Iraqi word meant "to lift" or "up."

Oz and Gerhard moved most of the prisoners to the lead bus and I pulled the last ten away to start loading the bags and blankets on the second bus. The drivers pulled up, stopped, and the passenger loading door swung open. I grabbed a handle on the rear emergency door and pulled it open to load from the rear forward. Each prisoner grabbed several handbags or blankets and began to load the rear section from floor to just below the windows. As I was getting one bus loaded, Gerhard was placing plastic handcuffs on each prisoner and handing him over to Oz, who was loading the other bus from rear to front. No one got preferred seating on this trip.

As this process was taking place, the other vehicles maneuvered into a convoy, leaving enough room for the buses to fall into a slot behind the lead vehicle. At some point during the morning, Lt. Marana got word that about half a dozen or so civilian tractor-trailer trucks would like to fall into our convoy for the trip back to Abu. The insertion of more vehicles meant that the arrangement would change to accommodate the additional trucks. The new order placed one gun truck in the lead, one in the center of the convoy, and one as a trail vehicle.

With the constant flow of supplies coming into southern Iraq through Kuwait, this was not unusual. The civilian contract truck drivers would often wait a few days after they arrived at Camp Bucca to hitch in with the military convoys heading north. These convoys could provide the cover and protection that the civilian tractor-trailers lacked. However, on this particular day, our convoy was beginning to look a little thin on the military side.

It was 0900 hours, and we were not yet on the road. We finally had everyone loaded on the bus and were ready to roll when the Lieutenant pulled the drivers into a huddle, minus the bus drivers and gave out the convoy briefing. Oz fell into the briefing to make sure we knew the plan as well. Oz returned and informed us that the Lieutenant wanted us to load the 9mm pistols into the lead Humvee with our rifles.

"What? You have got to be fucking kidding me," was Gerhard's immediate response, and I can't say that mine was any different.

"What's up with that, Oz?" I asked

"The lieutenant thinks that we have too many weapons in a crowded bus. We keep the shotguns, but the rifles and nines go in Gillman's truck." I stared at him and shook my head. "I know, I know," he said. "I asked the same question," he said, referring to what would happen if we had to fight our way out of something.

"What the fuck?" I said.

"The lieutenant felt we are a little outnumbered and he didn't want the detainees to have access to any extra weapons," Oz explained. Right or wrong, we didn't have much choice.

"Whatever," we mumbled and threw our heads back and handed him our weapons.

"Let's just get rolling," Oz said as he took them over to the Humvee.

"I don't care, it's going to get dark on us, and we're going to get caught on the road, no matter what," I uttered with some frustration and maybe a twinge of anger.

In retrospect, the lieutenant had a good point about the weapons and made a leadership decision that needn't be questioned. We knew we were transporting some very dangerous men. Some were Al-Qaeda, some Fedayeen, maintaining their loyalty to Saddam Hussein, and some just plain criminals. In any case, we could correctly assume that they were all were dangerous and would take any opportunity to kill us if it was given. Removing the extra weapons removed some of the opportunity.

Oz loaded the pistols with the other weapons in the rear of Gillman's truck and slammed the back hatch. He gave the latch one last thrust up, just to make sure it was locked, and then climbed onto the bus. Gerhard and I had already gotten aboard and made a brief security walk down the aisle as Oz took a seat at the front. The driver reached out and pulled a silver lever that shut the door. It looked like we were ready to move and head home.

Home is a very tricky word for soldiers and especially soldiers deployed overseas. When we typically think of home, we envision our family, where we keep our stuff, eat dinner, lay our head, and wake up for breakfast. Depending on the context of the sentence, and to whom we were talking, home mostly meant where we were from back in the States. However, when we were talking with one of our fellow soldiers, and were on a mission, home always meant Abu. Almost twelve solid months had passed since our feet first touched the ground at Abu Ghraib, and it was there where we lay our heads, ate our meals, and kept our stuff. It was also where our deployed family lived. The convoy started to move, and we were ready to head home.

Sunset at one of the western, interior towers at Abu Ghraib.

The road leading up to the ruins of Ur. The telephone poles
and antenna make for an interesting photo.

One of the two buses that were on the trip as it arrived on the morning of January 12, 2005.

Blackhawk helicopter on the landing pad at Abu Ghraib.

SSG. Adalwolf in the HUMMV on the January 12, 2005.

Left to right: Sgt. Wasserman, SSG. Osborne, and Sgt. Gerhard. Lt. Marana is sitting on the roof. January 11, 2005.

Back to Abu

GILLMAN'S HUMVEE TOOK THE LEAD. The large tires gripped into the soft sand, and he pulled through the chain link gate of the compound, heading towards the main gate out of the FOB. We fell in behind as the bus lurched forward and rocked slightly from side to side. The other bus loaded with bags followed in third position, and then several tractor-trailer rigs, and midway in the convoy, another gun truck, as we sometimes called the Humvees, fell into place. The remaining tractor-trailer rigs followed while the third Humvee was bringing up the rear.

It was approximately 0920, and we were finally on the road. The convoy drove through the gate of Camp Bucca and hit Highway 1 for Abu Ghraib. We were two hours late getting started, and there was no doubt that we were going to get caught on the road after dark. The best we'd be able to do was drive as hard as we could, stop briefly for fuel, and get as close as we could before the sun went down.

The hum of the engine permeated our senses again, as we slowly settled down for the twelve-hour trip. We were trying to find the most comfortable position that would also provide the best security advantage. Oz eventually decided to sit on the engine hump at the front facing toward the rear, with a clear view of the entire bus. That worked out well for a while, as it gave Gerhard and me both a full seat.

We scanned the occupants and saw the faces of our enemy. We saw the faces of old men, young men, and middle-aged men. Some may have done nothing at all, some may have been

Al-Qaeda, but almost all had been captured on the battlefield somewhere in Iraq. A few were not Iraqi, but represented other countries within the region, having come to fight the Americans. It seemed that everyone with an ax to grind came to Iraq to get a piece of the Great Satan and they were more than willing to die trying. The martyrdom philosophy was fine for most of the soldiers and especially the Marines fighting the battle every day, who were more than willing to kill all takers. But in the greater political scheme and in the eyes of the public, the battles won or lost wouldn't matter if the war wasn't finished soon.

A small amount of chatter traveled throughout the bus among the detainees, but most sat quietly, nervously shifting their weight from time to time to get comfortable. On occasion, a detainee would call us to complain that the plastic handcuffs were too tight and ask if we would loosen them. Standard operating procedure dictated that we check the restraints on a regular basis and ensure that they were not cutting off the circulation, but with few exceptions did we ever loosen the cuffs.

We were on the road about an hour when a prisoner began to complain about chest pains, a usual event. An English-speaking detainee started asking for help, saying his friend was having a heart attack. The callousness of our decisions may have seemed unwarranted to the casual observer, but it seemed every Iraqi with a sprained ankle or a headache was having a heart attack. Many times, I had pulled out a stethoscope and listened to a heart beating stronger than mine was, with no unusual fluctuations in rhythm, and a blood pressure of 120/70. I am not a doctor, but it was hard to believe anyone was having a heart attack with those vital signs.

With caution prevailing, I signaled to Oz to have the driver pull over. We were without radio communication, so we would have to hope that the lead vehicle got word from the trail vehicle or more likely, the turret gunner saw us stop and turned around. The driver pulled the bus to the edge of the highway, but not entirely off the road.

"Everybody stay seated," I said and motioned downward with my hand.

Then I motioned to the English speaker and the prisoner who appeared to be wincing in discomfort to come forward. I looked out ahead and it seemed that the lead vehicle had pulled over and was waiting to see what was going to happen. We were in the middle of nowhere with nothing but flat, open sand for miles and miles. Slowly, the two detainees made their way forward as the bus driver opened the door, and the three of us stepped out. The prisoner that was having the heart attack symptoms laid on the ground and began to moan. Regardless of my opinion, I was not able to determine his true condition. I sent Oz jogging back to the middle Humvee, which carried Staff Sergeant Adalwolf, one of the female medics in the battalion and very capable. She was always professional and never seemed to get overexcited and never lost her presence of mind.

On one particular chaotic morning during the summer I remember her coming into a violent uprising in the Ganci compound. We had more than a half dozen wounded. I was in the midst of trying to administer CPR to a fatally wounded detainee as Sgt. Adalwolf, who had gotten the call to respond, pulled up and saw the mess. I believe she could see the exhaustive effort I was putting into a dying man, with little positive result. She must have seen that nothing was going to work.

"Sgt. Wasserman," she said, as I continued. "Sgt. Wasserman." I looked back at her and could see in her eyes that she was calling the ball on this one. "It's okay to stop, Sergeant. I think this one is over," she said in an almost calming voice.

Sgt. Adalwolf told me a few days later that the man had indeed died and there was nothing anyone could have done that would have changed the outcome. It would take me ten years to tell her, but I appreciated her stoic demeanor and her soothing voice on that early morning nightmare. Every once in a while I could see a bit of a sense of humor in her eyes that let me know that she was not taking anything too seriously and the place had not broken her spirit.

She approached the bus and in her naturally calm and casual fashion and asked, "What's up, Sgt. Wasserman?"

"Sgt. Adalwolf, they tell me that this guy is having a heart attack."

"Probably not, but let's take a look at him anyway." She took his pulse, listened to his heart, and said he was probably just dehydrated and feeling anxious. All of which were true. Many times, we found that the prisoners would not drink enough water, and no one knew why. They seemed to prefer an IV of saline solution. It was a free fill-up without having to drink water.

After a few minutes of idle talk and making sure the detainee was okay, Sgt. Adalwolf concluded that it was as she had said earlier, dehydration and anxiety. Drink water and calm down was the medicine of the day. We boarded the bus again and got ourselves resituated. The door squeaked shut and we gave the bus driver the signal to get moving. Gradually he pulled back onto the hard surface and regained convoy speed. At the same time, the lead vehicle also pulled onto the highway and began to accelerate ahead of us. This was just another delay in what had been a stumbling morning so far. It was a little after 1030, and the goal was to keep the convoy steadily moving and get back as soon as possible.

Mere minutes after getting back on the road again, we heard an all too familiar call from a detainee in the rear of the bus, "Mister, Mister."

"What now?" Oz stood up and yelled to the back of the bus.

"Mister, please. The handcuffs are too tight," and a detainee lifted his hands into the air.

"Shut up! They're fine," Gerhard responded in his usual loud and forceful fashion.

Out of caution mostly, Oz walked down the center aisle to check the man's cuffs, and I asked him, "You know they're okay, why do you do this?"

In a nonchalant tone, Oz said, "It's going to be a long trip. I just need to know from time to time they're secure."

I gave him a fist bump and said, "Okay. . .Good deal man." That was good enough for me.

As the convoy continued a steady pace northward, we discussed some of the mistrust we had for our passengers, and it may have been just a gut feeling, but it existed. We were sure that they didn't have the best of intentions planned.

"Hey, guys," I said as I leaned into Oz and Gerhard. "I know these bastards are setting us up for something. I can just feel it, and you guys know it, too. I don't know what it is yet, but it's a long straight shot back to Abu, and I just feel something is hinky about it all. I damn sure don't trust these drivers either. We have another eight or nine hours on the road, and they have nothing better to do than to concoct something stupid."

Oz agreed, "You're right, Wass. We don't know these drivers or any of the thugs in here. We could all end up with our heads on a stick"

Still angry about the morning, Gerhard started to rant, "And putting our weapons in Gillman's truck, that was jacked up, and leaving us with just the shotguns. What will they do for us? And no comm's either?

We didn't dwell on it and we didn't need to express what we felt in order to understand it, but once we cleared the air, we accepted this mission as it was. "Hey, it is what it is," Oz replied.

"Yep, it is." I said.

Now that all of the whining seemed to be over, it appeared that everyone had settled in for the remainder of the trip. Our gripes and moans now turned to lighter subjects and the casual talk of what to do when we got home. This particular discussion of home meant real home, wheels up home; real food, real bed and real life home.

The steady hum of the engine, periods of silence, and the lack of any real scenery allowed a somewhat unfamiliar calmness to set in. It was not exactly relaxing, but not entirely threatening or filled with anticipation, either.

The silence and calm was broken with conversation turning to what to do after Iraq. We decided that we should get together on this exact date the next year. We would all get together at some place equidistant to all of us and hang out together for a few days. We thought aloud for a minute about where we all lived and randomly decided to meet in Gatlinburg, Tennessee, on January 12, 2006.

In order to seal the deal officially, I suggested, "When we get back, we'll sign a five-dinar bill. We'll all keep one, and, what the heck. . . let's give one to Vacho, as well," and we roughly agreed to stay in touch and get together at least once a year.

The chatter among the prisoners in Arabic continued. The hum of the road and endless miles of open nothingness was interrupted again as the convoy began to slow down for a fuel stop. This particular fuel point did not appear to have the zigzag type of entrance from our direction or maybe due to the fact we had detainees with us, we passed straight through. Regardless, it was easy in and easy out, and much faster than the day before.

The engine changed its pitch as it slowed, and the long line of vehicles began to bunch up. It would barely be enough time to stretch our legs and hit the porta-john, but it was a break. In an attempt at being humane, I would try to get some prisoners off the bus and give them a chance at the restroom. I started with a few of the older men who seemed like they were in the most discomfort and in all probability needed it more than the others. I was also fighting the time crunch. The lieutenant did not want to stay any longer than necessary. We were already behind schedule and with just about three hours of daylight remaining, we almost certainly had five hours or more of driving.

In true Iraqi fashion, these guys took forever to take a piss. Once they had drained their bladders, they had to remove their shoes and wash their feet, face, hands, and ears—every time. It was a religious ritual that had to be done. Regardless of the reason, it took forever.

"*Yalla, Yalla!*" I screamed. "Come on, can we hurry it up?"

I was able to get two or three detainees off the bus and actually get to the restroom, but the vast majority had to continue to hold it or use a water bottle. In mere minutes, we were moving again. The convoy pulled away from the fuel point, and the lead vehicle pulled ahead and stopped for a moment. Lt. Bodiker opened his door; stepped out with one foot on the road, and looked back to make sure the rest of the convoy was falling in. Satisfied, he sat back inside, and the door of the Humvee bounced shut as the vehicle pulled away and began to speed up.

The buses followed, but the speed did not come quite as rapidly. We stood up and looked through the rear window to see the second bus and the rest of the convoy trailing in a long line. We were grouped tight at first, but as we drove several miles, the line began to spread out to reasonable intervals. The Arabic chatter slowed, and the detainees often whispered to each other in a way that made them look suspicious, even if they had done nothing wrong.

"You know we're going to get caught on the road after dark; the question is where," I said to both Oz and Gerhard.

"And these nasty bastards are just too fidgety," Gerhard said.

"Oh, hell yes, they are," Oz concurred.

Gerhard finally made the point that all of us undeniably had been thinking when he said, "Somebody fucked this one up. This isn't a mission we should be doing. Seventeen of these Coalition-killing rat bastards are coming back, why?"

Reliable rumor in the soldier grapevine was that the original seventeen were released to Camp Bucca by mistake before they were thoroughly interrogated, and their names had popped up again. Whatever the reason, the intelligence officers wanted them back. We had no way of knowing which seventeen of the forty-two were the high value detainees, but it didn't matter. We treated them all the same, with suspicion.

Oz made another sweep of the aisle and noticed that an old man was trying to cut his flex-cuffs on the ashtray on the back of the seat in front of him.

"Hey, numb nuts, stop that!" he shouted. Then he yelled back to us, "Some of these guys are trying to cut their cuffs off with the ash tray."

"Oh man, these bastards have got something up their sleeve," Gerhard said, and he walked back to where Oz was standing.

"Hey, stupid, stop it," Gerhard screamed. "Let's zip this guy up again." Oz pulled another set of cuffs out of his cargo pocket to re-secure the detainee's hands. Not entirely oblivious to the fact that a twelve-hour trip with your hands restrained could be uncomfortable, I tried to find some humane rationale for the actions and to empathize with the detainee's situation, but we weren't going to ride with these guys unsecure, no matter how uncomfortable it was for them.

"I'm sure the cuffs are just damned rough, and when they have to pee in the bottle, it's not easy."

Oz sat back down and replied, "I know, but if one gets loose? I don't trust them."

"Not a one," Gerhard added.

"You're right," I said. "I know if they got a chance they would cut our throats right here in the seat and throw us out the door."

Oz knew and agreed, "You're damn right they would."

Gerhard, the most edgy, leaned into us and said in a low voice, "I know I said it before, but I don't trust these nasty-ass bus drivers, either. Where did they pull these two guys from anyway, does anybody know?"

"And what the hell happened to the original buses and drivers? We don't know what these mutts are saying or if they are colluding with the detainees."

It was hard to disagree, but we were soldiers and the mission was what it was. We had to play the hand we had, not the hand we wished we had. On this day, we were tasked with guarding these detainees for a few more hours, so that was what we did. We figured when we reached Abu and turned them over, it would be just another mission completed, another convoy of the many already driven, and they would be someone else's problem. We didn't have much option either way, but we didn't want to stop Gerhard from complaining. It was our small form of entertainment for the time being, and it was funny to watch him go off on the subject.

The brightness of the daylight gave way to twilight. And as if someone had a rope on the sun and yanked it straight down below the horizon, it became dark. The volume of talk among the detainees continued to cycle up and down, but was always a simmering murmur. Curiosity about their location seemed to be important. The lights were off inside the bus, and small noises were muffled by the hum of the engine and the steady bump of the road. The prisoners on occasion tried to pull back the curtains that draped the windows, and we constantly had to shout warnings to keep them closed. It was dark, and we were beginning to feel the length of the trip.

"How far to Abu Ghraib, mister?" one detainee asked.

With a sharp voice Gerhard replied, "None of your damn business."

The day before, about an hour or an hour and a half away from Abu, we had crossed three bridges as we left for Camp Bucca. Each bridge had been blown up either during the initial invasion or in subsequent attacks by insurgents. The U.S. military had replaced each bridge with an engineered Army bridge. They were meant to be temporary, were single lane and allowing a single vehicle at a time to cross. Traffic that far out was minimal and patrolling convoys had kept the insurgent activity down. Constant air patrols had also been effective in limiting the number of IEDs on major arteries overall. We were, however, closing back in on the Sunni Triangle, if not already there, and the highway at night was not the place we wanted to be caught.

Our order in the convoy was the number two vehicle, with one Humvee in front of us as the lead. Behind us was the other bus, which was empty except for the belongings of the prisoners.

We approached the first bridge and the lead Humvee slowed as it got closer to the narrow structure and carefully proceeded over it. It pulled up at least one hundred yards beyond the bridge, stopped, and waited until the remaining convoy could make the crossing. After the first Humvee had crossed, we approached the bridge and slowly rolled the front tires over the metal ramp that formed a small bump at each end. The driver gave it just enough gas to pull the bus onto the metal ramp and crossed slowly as the convoy began to bunch up behind us. You could hear the metal from the structure squeak and creak as we rolled down the opposing ramp and fell in behind the lead vehicle. It started to pull further down the road, never fully stopped and allowed the lagging vehicles to catch up.

We accelerated back up to convoy speed, and it appeared that everyone made the crossing safely. Inside the bus, chatter and conversation amongst detainees seemed to pick up. It was apparent they knew we were getting closer to Abu. We reacted in an opposite manner and spoke less, individually trading sparse comments here and there.

Gerhard broke the semi-silence and said, "I'm ready for this mission to be over. I want to get off this bus, get some real food, and go to bed."

Oz seconded it with, "You and me both."

I glanced at Oz and Gerhard and said, "You know, I'm ready to go home, too. I mean home, home. I think we've been to every corner of this country in the last year, done everything we've been asked to do, we have gone every place we were told to go, and maybe a few places we weren't told to go. I know we've been shot at enough. I want to defend Fort Living Room next."

Both Oz and Gerhard agreed. "I'm with you there," Gerhard said.

Almost without notice, we were at the second bridge. We crossed in similar fashion as the first. The convoy picked up speed and continued the drive toward Abu. Looking out through the front glass, we saw the faint light of the Humvee in front of us and whatever amount of road our headlights allowed. We were no more than twenty or twenty-five minutes away from the last bridge and thick anticipation of coming to the end of a long trip hung heavy in the air. Whispers drifted between the detainees, but actual talk was almost non-existent.

The three of us had gone nearly silent and were just keeping ourselves alert for the final minutes of this trip. One of us was constantly watching the road ahead and as expected, we saw the brake lights of the lead vehicle flare up. We closed the gap between the first Humvee as it began to make its way over the last bridge. The Humvee rolled off the other end and we slowed down, putting our front wheels on the ramp. We watched as the Humvee pulled about thirty-five or forty yards beyond the end of the bridge and into the darkness, waiting. Again, we heard the familiar creak of the large vehicle on the metal system as we slowly moved across. Within just yards of rolling down the small ramp at the opposite side, the bus abruptly stopped. The white noise of the engine ceased. For a brief second, it was absolutely quiet.

"What the hell!" Oz shouted as he sprung to his feet directing his attention to the bus driver. The halt caught Gerhard's and my attention at about the same time as Gerhard exploded, "I knew it! It's a damn setup! I knew these rat bastards were up to something!"

The bus driver appeared to be surprised and began trying to restart the engine. We heard only the grinding of the starter turning over without the engine firing off. Oz, the closest to the driver by less than twelve inches, pulled his shotgun to his shoulder and shouted to the driver, "You need to get this bus started and *started now!*"

"I'm sorry, mister," the driver said nervously. "I don't know what is the matter. It won't start." He continued to turn the ignition switch, grinding the starter with no result.

"I cannot see what is wrong," the driver tried to explain.

I was between Oz and Gerhard as Oz told the driver, "Do not turn on the inside lights." And almost as if it was planned, and blatantly disregarding the command, the driver hit the switch, and the inside of the bus illuminated with white incandescence.

I turned toward the driver and shouted to him, "Lights out!"

Oz pumped his shotgun once, slamming a round home and said, "Turn off the lights, or I'm going to blow your damn head off!" The driver quickly slapped the switch, and the lights went out.

No more than ninety seconds had passed since the bus came to a stop. Simultaneously, as the bus driver had initially disobeyed Oz's command, the detainees had started trying to pull back the small drapes that covered the windows in an effort to see outside, to see where they were or, as we believed, what was going to happen next.

Gerhard, already further into the aisle of the bus, had his weapon to his shoulder. He screamed, "Leave the windows alone! Do not pull the curtains open!"

Crouched and crowded, I had my weapon to my shoulder at the low ready. "Hands down, hands down! Keep away from the windows!" I shouted.

Oz continued to press the bus driver to get the engine started. Again, the driver turned the ignition switch, and the starter was turned over, but nothing happened. The driver stopped and, turned the switch again and unexpectedly, without jerking, it seemed that he had slowly released the clutch enough to allow the starter to turn the engine over, while in gear, and the wheels moved a few rotations. The front of the bus rolled off the end of the bridge, with enough momentum to roll far enough away to allow a vehicle to pass behind our tail end. We cleared the bridge. Oz, with his weapon lowered, was at the driver's back, forcibly urging him, "You need to start this bus. It was running a minute ago; get it running again!"

The lead Humvee, which had monitored us through their mirrors, backed up a few yards and stopped. Lt. Bodiker swung open the heavy door of the Humvee, got out, and quickly began to walk back towards the bridge and us. He more than likely could see that something was wrong, and as he got closer, he could hear the grinding of the starter. The driver, now very nervous, pulled the lever of the door to swing it open. Lt. Bodiker, appearing tired and angry, stuck his head inside far enough to be heard and said "You need to get this bus started and rolling right now. You have two minutes!"

Gerhard almost unaware the lieutenant had made his way back was commanding the prisoners in his most profane language not to look out the windows, "Get your hands down you nasty bastards, hands down!" He turned to me and said, "I knew these bastards were going to pull something!"

I responded to Lt. Bodiker's frustration in my own irritated manner, "Sir, we're not mechanics, but we're working it out." I turned to Oz and said, "We've got to work out a plan and fast, or we're screwed."

Lt. Bodiker had no response, turned, quickly walked back to his vehicle, and sat back inside. I believe he understood the situation as well as we did and had enough confidence in us that he knew we would solve the problem, one way or another. Moments later, the lead Humvee pulled farther up the road, virtually out of sight and waited with blackout lights vaguely visible. The second bus, directly behind us, had pulled forward, edged past the rear end and stopped alongside, angling the front end slightly to the side of the road. The driver, a relative of the driver of our broken carriage, had walked over and the two of them began to discuss the problem in Arabic, signaling with their hands what seemed to be an unsolvable mechanical problem. Again, the driver turned the key in the ignition, and we heard the sound of the starter as it continued to grind.

Approximately four or five minutes had passed since we first stopped. We had about a fifteen-meter gap between the two buses, and both sets of headlights shined off into endless darkness. Some of the detainees that were closest to the driver wanted to offer their two-cent's worth on the situation, and we quickly halted the discussion.

"Quiet, no talking," I said, as shotguns remained at the low ready and Gerhard stayed poised towards the rear.

I turned my head and said in a normal tone, "Back up, Oz," and he moved backwards down the steps and stood on the road. I backed up and stood on the first step inside the door, closest to the driver, who stayed behind the wheel. The other driver had stepped back into the road and stood nearby, but slightly behind Oz. I pulled my weapon in close, turned to the other driver, and told him, "Go back to your bus and sit down."

He said, "But, Mister."

I interrupted him mid-sentence, "Go back to your bus, sit down, and do it now."

Oz, understanding that something had just clicked asked, as we were looking at each other dead in the eyes, "What do you have in mind, Wass? What's the plan here?"

"We're going to move these guys from this bus over to the other, one at a time, quickly, and leave this piece of crap right here in the road," I said. "We'll stack them on each other if we have to, but everybody gets into the bus.

Oz pulled his lips tight, nodded his head in agreement, and said, "We're going to be spread kind of thin."

"I know. We sure could use another gun, but it is what it is."

Gerhard had moved to the front of the bus next to the driver. Now the three of us were bunched up at the door opening with Oz standing on the road.

"You got it, Gerhard?" I said making sure he understood what was getting ready to happen.

Gerhard said with a sense of urgency, "These Haji bastards have been cutting their cuffs on those ash trays again. Half of them are un-fucking-done; let's do something."

I answered, "I have some more of the flex-cuffs in my cargo pocket, but this is what we'll do." I looked at Gerhard and said, "You stay up there next to the driver and pull these guys up and off one at a time. Check their hands and give me a shout about what's going on with their hands. Then push them down to me."

Gerhard nodded and said, "Roger that," and swung his shotgun down to his side and slightly behind, easily within reach, but not inhibiting.

I then looked at Oz and told him, "You go over to the other bus and stand at the corner so I can see you. I'll zip up the ones that need it and then push them over to you. If this goes bad, fall back to the edge of the road. Got it?" We each gave the other a nod, and I stepped off the bottom step onto the road. Our nearest gun truck was at least fifty yards ahead of us, waiting. Anyone else who may have been able to help was on the other side of the bridge and was unable to see exactly what was unfolding.

We stood there in the road and at the door of our broken-down bus, the three of us hastily pulling together this plan to get rolling again and out of danger. Oz looked at Gerhard and me and said, "You're the only two people I trust, just you guys, no one else." Just as Oz began to step away with his shotgun in hand, a soldier appeared from around the front of the bus, cutting across the headlights, and walked up to our taut group.

He wore the familiar desert camouflage uniform with a SAW slung in front at the ready and a patch on his shoulder. He simply asked, "Do you fellows need a hand?"

Oz and I were somewhat startled; we did not expect anyone to come walking around and appear from the front or the rear. It was certainly dark, but enough of the residual light from the headlights told us that we were still in the middle of nowhere.

Surprised, I asked, "Where did you come from?" The soldier nodded in a general direction and said, "Over there." I gave a quick peek around to the front, but I didn't see a thing and thought to myself, *over where?*

"Okay," I said. I was not in a position to question the specifics or check references. I was glad he was there, and at the time, I didn't really care where he had come from or how he got there. Santa Claus could have dropped him off and it wouldn't have mattered to me. He was willing to help, and that was all I truly needed to know. In quick Army language, I spelled out the situation to him and asked if he could pull security while we made the transfer of detainees from one bus to the next.

The soldier looked at us and said, "No problem."

I looked up toward Gerhard and told him, "Okay, let's do this," and I moved a couple paces back from the door. Oz shifted to his position at the front corner of the second bus and prepared to receive the detainees as they were moved toward him. Because of the darkness and his need to move in and out of door opening, Oz had handed his weapon to the fourth soldier who had curiously appeared at the precise moment we needed him.

The soldier pulled the shotgun sling over one arm and shoulder, and then pushed the weapon slightly to the rear similar to the way Gerhard had done. I caught Oz's position in the corner of my eye and turned my attention back toward Gerhard and our mission. My back was to both Oz and the fourth soldier. I heard the familiar click of the slide being pulled back and closed on the SAW, a typical reflex action that a soldier will sometimes do when readying a weapon. However, on that night, I believed it was an intentional act to give a distinct sound of reinforcement, to all who could hear and to let everyone know he was there. I didn't know this mystery soldier from Adam, but he was dressed like us, acted like us, and had a machine gun. We had to trust him with our lives.

"First one, Wass . . . undone," Gerhard shouted out as the first detainee stepped off of the bottom step and took a step or two toward me.

"Hands," I told him in what we called a command level voice. He pulled back the sleeves of his yellow jumpsuit and presented a broken pair of flex-cuffs on his wrist. I quickly slid a new pair over his hands and pulled the tails just a little tighter than before. At this point, we could not afford to have them broken again and we did not want anything to encourage the Hajis to go brave on us.

"Oz, one coming to you," I said, directing the detainee with an outstretched left arm.

"Next . . . he's good," Gerhard shouted down, as an indication that the prisoner's cuffs were still intact. At this point, maybe because of knowing that the detainee's hands were good, I looked at his face and saw an expression of surprise mixed with bewilderment and disappointment. His eyes had moved off to my side and picked up the fourth soldier who was standing behind me with his weapon slung at the ready. The soldier shifted his weight and turned to Oz as if he were making sure that the prisoner saw that he was being covered.

"Oz, coming to you," I said, and again I directed another detainee to the second bus.

"Next . . . undone," Gerhard shouted, as he sent the next one down the steps. The detainee had his hands in front of him. This time I watched his face, and his eyes caught the fourth soldier behind me, standing watch. Again, I saw bewilderment. I repositioned the new set of zip-ties on his wrists and pulled them snug.

"Oz, one more coming to ya," I said, and I directed the prisoner as before.

Oz grabbed each one by the elbow and walked them the few steps to the door, followed them up the steps, and commanded them to move as far back to the rear as possible and sit down. The bus had already been about twenty percent full with the detainees' personal belongings. Now we were going to stuff everybody into an even smaller space. He had some of them sitting on top of the luggage and blankets or stuffed into the seats. The upside of this situation was that we were within forty-five minutes of reaching Abu.

"Wass . . . next one undone," Gerhard shouted.

"Oz . . . coming to ya," I said, and this scene played out repeatedly for all forty-two detainees in a steady rapid-fire sequence as they were transferred. Nearly half of them had their flex-cuffs broken and their hands free. Almost all the detainees that stepped off the bus that night saw the stranger. I am sure they wondered from where he had come. Their reaction registered with me, but I said nothing and kept my observations to myself for the time being.

It had been approximately fifteen minutes, plus or minus, since we had stopped. As the last prisoner stepped onto the second bus, Gerhard cleared the seats and walked down the steps. We rallied at the door of the running bus, as the fourth soldier walked over and handed Oz back his shotgun. The two drivers had a brief discussion in Arabic. It appeared the driver of the stalled transport was hesitating, but he decided to jump in with us and not hang out on the road alone. I am guessing that he believed he was better off coming along, and he would more than likely come back in the morning.

The four of us quickly said our good-byes. We shook the soldier's hand.

"Thank you . . . big time, dude, this could have turned ugly on us fast," I told him.

Oz added, "We owe you one, and really—thanks!"

True to form, Gerhard just gave the guy a solid fist pound, threw him a look of gratitude, and moved out. We boarded and moved into the center of the aisle. I stood closest to the driver because I was the last to board. I signaled the driver that we needed to get moving again. Each of us were now watching and on alert for any additional surprises. Gerhard had his weapon tucked in tight at the low ready and kept his eyes on the detainees, some of which were now sitting on the floor. Oz and I peered out the front window to make sure the dim lights of the lead Humvee were still visible. We also paid close attention to the driver as he prepared to move.

The driver shifted the transmission into gear, eased off the clutch just enough to make the cumbersome vehicle lurch forward, and started to ease into a roll. Just as the bus began to move, Oz and I crouched down to give the fourth soldier a wave, a gesture of acknowledgement, like when someone lets you into traffic. We bent over and stared through the windows to find that our friend was gone. My eyes rapidly scanned the area where we had just been moving about, but I didn't see him. There was almost enough residual light to make out a human figure if it was there. The next vehicle in the convoy, seeing our taillights flicker, had moved onto the bridge and was casting light on the road from our rear.

"Oz, where *did* he go?" I asked.

"I don't know . . . where did he go?" Oz also quickly searched the area through the driver's window and through the door, but he didn't see him either. I looked at the bus driver who stared back at me. He saw, he knew, but he said nothing.

"*Weird*," I said to myself as we began to pick up speed and close back in on the lead vehicle. Soon, many sets of headlights began to appear behind us as the remaining vehicles made their way over the bridge and caught up with the convoy.

Our adrenaline was rushing, and we were keyed-up. What we believed may have been planned to happen, did not happen. For the next twenty minutes, the talk and whispers had halted to a dead silence. Except for the low moan of the engine, a person could hear a pin drop on the floor. Oz, Gerhard, and I just glanced at each other and communicated through a few facial expressions. Something had changed.

Passing Through

WITH THE NORMAL TALK AMONG the prisoners all but stopped, a small trickle of barely audible words spaced with silence was all that could be heard. Once the bus was rolling again, our convoy still had approximately forty-minutes of travel time until we would roll into Abu. Everyone aboard sat packed and very still. It was both unnerving and a relief at the same time.

Was something waiting for us the next mile up the road? Was that breakdown a planned event that had been interrupted? Were the bus driver's conspirators in a failed plot to help the detainees escape? Stranger things had happened before, and there was no reason not to believe that this incident was planned. Finally, I broke the quiet of the moment. In a low whisper, I asked, "Gerhard, where did that guy come from?"

Gerhard replied, "I don't know, Wass. You saw him about the same time that I did."

"Was there a checkpoint at that location?" I asked.

Again, Gerhard had no real explanation, but replied, "Who has ever heard of a one-man checkpoint in the middle of nowhere? Maybe something was there, but all I saw was blackness."

I turned to Oz and asked, "Could a patrol have been coming through the area?"

Oz said, "A one man patrol, out there? It was too dark to see anyone or anything else."

I looked at both of them and said, "That was a little unusual guys, really strange." I could see the question marks in their eyes. But nothing came to mind that gave us a good answer. I don't think anyone would have ever expected the mission would have such a strange finale or could have predicted what happened. However, we weren't complaining. The nature of the business was to expect the unexpected, and we just kept doing what we were assigned to do, guarding the prisoners until we got back to Abu Ghraib.

Through the dim glow of the dash lights, we could faintly see each other's faces. Each of us held our weapons close as the final minutes ticked away. Possibly the most memorable event of our tour had just taken place, and what made it significant was the fact it was a non-event. What could have happened didn't happen. We contemplated the possibilities as we saw the floodlights glare through the windows. We were home, and though we didn't know it at the time, it was indeed our final mission.

The lead vehicle rolled through the main checkpoint into Abu Ghraib. The bus with its high center of gravity, rolled aggressively to one side as it made the sharp turn from the road through the checkpoint area and inside the gate. On each side of the entry control point were two solidly fortified fighting positions with several well-armed Marines. This was ECP East. Once past this point, we knew we were inside the protection of the walls, but we were anxious and the job was not quite complete.

The bus twisted through concrete barriers that lined the inner roads of Abu, and the convoy began to separate, going to different destinations within the FOB Our bus and at least one Humvee headed to the IHA. The IHA was where all of the prisoners were processed and held until a determination could be made on who was going where. Most would be sent to the outside camps, now broken down and named into levels of detention. Level 1 Alpha being the least restrictive to the detainees. The seventeen that created the mission may have had other destinations, but that would be determined later on. The in-processing could take a day or two depending on the number of prisoners that were brought in at a time. Lt. Bodiker had all of the paperwork on each prisoner, and this information was maintained throughout the prisoner's period of detention. If the truth were known, it is still most likely maintained somewhere, even today.

The lead Humvee whipped around in a large gravel lot in front of the IHA as Gerhard leaned down to direct the driver to follow the Humvee and told him where to park. We stopped. I signaled the driver to open the door and I said to Gerhard and Oz, "I'm going to grab the guys inside, and we'll get this thing wrapped up as soon as I can drag them out here."

I walked towards a large plywood door at about the same time that Lt. Bodiker was getting out of the Humvee with the paperwork. Sgt. Garner also stepped out, put her pack on the ground, stretched, and stood briefly, doing nothing.

As I walked back outside with a trail of soldiers following me, Gerhard was having the prisoners dismount, line up, and kneel to the ground with their hands cupped behind their heads and was cutting off their flex-cuffs. Oz maintained his station inside the bus, searching every seat and making sure everyone was out. Gerhard had his hands full, but there was usually a small flurry of activity in and around the IHA, with soldiers coming and going for different reasons. The Grand Central Station-like atmosphere added a sense of security as well as a sense of confusion as Gerhard managed the detainees with a good amount of skill and rock solid authority.

I approached Sgt. Garner and asked, "Hey, can you help Gerhard out?"

Garner, looking a bit puzzled replied, "With what?"

All of this caught me in a bad moment. Angrily, I snapped back with, "Guarding the prisoners, Garner," and handed her my shotgun. I walked over to the bus and told Oz, "Hey, dude, Gillman has pulled off with our gear; I'm going to try to track him down."

Oz replied, "We'll be here waiting for you."

I walked away and glanced back to see Sgt. Garner handing the weapon back over to Oz as the other MPs came out to begin the processing. Sarcastically, I thought, *yeah, she is real Hooah.*

In retrospect, maybe she had done nothing wrong. She just happened to be standing next to the Humvee at about the time I walked by, and I allowed a little fatigue to get the best of me. I was pissed that all of our gear, including backpacks, sleeping bags, etc., was still stowed in Gillman's Humvee, which had pulled away after it dropped Sgt. Garner and Lt. Bodiker off, but still I felt she could have helped out a little.

Just as we were getting our situation straightened, Sgt. Major Vacho walked up and said, in his friendly Wisconsin accent, "Well, I see you boys have made it back."

Oz replied, "Yes, Sergeant Major, we did."

The usual small talk was being bantered about when I asked him, "Sergeant Major, have the incoming units taken over and made it out into the areas of operation yet?"

He replied, "I don't know, Wass. I know they're coming in, but I don't think they're out picking up the mission yet. I do know that the 18th MP Brigade will be taking over for us here soon. Why do you ask?"

"Well, Sergeant Major, a little over an hour ago, as we were coming home, the bus broke down, and we had the strangest thing happen." We gave him the *Reader's Digest* version of the story, and he listened almost in disbelief.

Sergeant Vacho took his helmet off, amazed at our little story. "No kidding?" he said. "Well, did you get a name or a unit? Maybe we can drop a good word to his CO or something."

"No, Sergeant Major, we didn't. He was dressed like us, and he had a SAW, and that was all we cared about at the time," I replied.

We continued to sort through our mangle of gear and weapons, checked our ammunition, re-packed it, and talked with Sergeant Major Vacho a bit more. He continued to laugh at more of our tales, listened to our gripes, and told us that we had wrapped the year up in style. We had done a good job and he was proud of us. At some point, I pulled out the Iraqi dinars with Saddam Hussein's picture on one side.

"Hey, I think we wanted to remember this day, right?" I asked and began signing four of the bills and wrote the date, Jan. 12, 2005, on each one. I gave one each to Oz, Gerhard, and Sgt. Major Vacho, and I kept one for myself. We hung out there in the floodlights with the sergeant major a few more minutes, watching the prisoners as they were processed and slowly we felt the weight of the long day collapsing on us.

Gerhard, ready to relax, pulled up his pack and walked off, heading to his room. "I'll see you guys tomorrow," he said as he disappeared behind buildings and darkness.

"Later, guy," I said, and I gave him a nod as I pulled my own pack up to my shoulder.

"It is almost over for us, guys," the sergeant major commented.

"Yep," I said, and I paused. "I would love to reminisce with you some more, but we're beat, Sergeant Major. All I want to do right now is get a shower and lay my head down."

"Yeah, yuse guys get some rest, and I'll see you in the morning," he said, as Oz and I headed off to our crumbled rooms of refuge.

As if I had not even left, I was pounding my feet up the concrete stairs to my home away from home. I could hear the metal scrape as Oz opened the door of his small room. I opened my own squeaky metal door and slung my pack into its spot on the floor, near the head of my bunk. Instinctively, I reached for a place on the wall and hit the light switch. As the light came on, I saw a mouse run across the floor to the other side of the room. I said to myself, *well, mister rat, you stay on that side of the room, and I'll stay on my side, and we'll be good for the night.* My other roommate was gone, presumably at work. He and I worked opposite shifts, which allowed each of us to get some rest without disturbing the other. It was almost 2200 hours Iraqi time, and I had not gotten much sleep the night before. Although the trip was not physically demanding its mental workload had sapped my energy.

I had two more things I needed to do before I lay my head on the pillow. First, was to get a shower and slip into my comfortable green scrubs. The second was to give my wife a call. I leaned my rifle against the wall close to my bunk, peeled off my ballistic vest, and grounded it next to my rifle. I neatly stacked my helmet on top. Even though our room was located in a partially destroyed building that used to be a dusty prison, infested with rodents and with few creature comforts, it still had order to it. I was not feeling hungry and decided to skip dinner. I had plenty of snacks and cans of tuna stored under my bunk if the urge to eat hit me. A cold bottle of water and some cheese nibs was all I needed as I pulled my boots off and placed them under the bunk.

I took off my uniform and stuffed it into a laundry bag. Tomorrow, I'd get a clean uniform, a reward I'd give to myself for a long couple of days. Typically, we all tried to get at least three days wear out of one uniform, sometimes maybe more. They got a little salty and a little dirty, but everyone smelled the same, so it wasn't overwhelmingly noticed. I jumped into my green scrubs I used as pajamas, grabbed my towel, shaving kit, rifle, and pistol and headed to the same shower trailer that had been hit with shrapnel a month or so before. It was hard not to think about that event with the holes still visible in the walls. I let the warm, soapy water rinse the grime of the day off of me and exhaled the tension, I brushed my teeth and looked into the mirror, satisfied at the job well done. I was clean again and happy, walking back to my room to grab my satellite phone and complete my final task of the evening

Usually, at some point during the middle of the phone call Sergeant 1st Class Groomes would wander from his cave wearing a purple robe, a towel over one shoulder and his shaving bag under one arm, also heading to the shower. He resembled a black Liberace as he walked out to the trailer each evening. And sure enough: right on time, Sgt. Groomes walked by and gave me the usual greeting as I sat down and started dialing the number.

"Say good evening to Mrs. Wasserman, Sgt. Wasserman," Groomes shouted out to me.

"Will do, Sergeant Groomes," I said acknowledging his presence.

The satellite phone required a clear, unobstructed sky to get a signal. I would usually grab a fold-up chair and sit out near the center of the quad close to the trailers to make my calls. I pushed the green, dimly lit buttons on the phone and waited for the ringing sound on the other end. Again, due to the distance and the transmission to the satellite, we had the six-second delay in communication.

"Hello," I could hear my wife answer the phone.

I tried to reply, "Hello."

"Hello, Hello," Nadaleane said, as if no one was answering, then came an ear piercing, "Sweetie pie!" after she heard my first, delayed hello. "Baby, I have missed you!" she screamed into the phone. "It is so good to hear your voice again."

I waited a few seconds before I answered and allowed our conversation to get in-sync and then I said, "I have missed you too, baby, but I just called you last night."

"I know," she said, "but you know how much I miss you and how much I look forward to hearing your voice. It puts me to bed every night and lets me know that you're okay. I need it, Gerit. I won't rest well without hearing your voice. I need to know you're okay."

"I'm okay, sweetie pie and I know you wait for me to call. I have just been busy with work, but I wanted to tell you we had something really strange happen tonight," I said hoping not to upset her fragile calmness.

With some concern in her voice she asked, "Oh, what happened, sweetheart?"

"Nothing bad," I immediately said to put her mind at ease. "You're not going to believe this." And I began to tell her the story of the night's events at the bridge and how a fourth man, a stranger, but a soldier like us, showed up at just the right moment. I gave her the essentials and not so much about the military mission. I waited for a reply and I heard a pause, a breath taken.

"Hello, Nadaleane?" I asked.

"I am here, sweetie pie," she said, her voice almost tearful. "You're not going to believe this, Gerit, but I had a feeling about your trip all day, today. Something inside of me was worried and fearful. I've been praying all day for your safety and for your buddies' safety."

"I know, sweetie pie, you always do," I said in a somewhat discarding fashion.

She paused again, and I could sense her waiting to choose her words carefully. Using the satellite phone was expensive, and I was inpatient. "What is it, Nadaleane?" Tell me, urging her for more than what she was saying.

"Gerit, I'm sure that was an angel that came to help you tonight."

I was stunned at her explanation; I could only utter a single word, "What?"

Pausing, so not to dismiss her feelings or her faith. "I don't know about all that, but his timing was pretty good," I said.

She repeated with some certainty, "It was an angel, Gerit, believe me."

Again, sloughing it off, I said, "Nadaleane, I didn't see any halo or white glow. To me, he was a soldier like us, and he had a weapon."

"Sweetheart," she said. "They don't show up like on TV. They show up the way you need them. Trust me, it was an angel. They walk the earth like you and me. He came the way you needed him, and you needed another soldier."

I gave in to her assertion, knowing that she had called this one right in most respects. We did need another soldier. I said, "Okay, baby, I trust you, but I'm tired, and I would like to call it a day. Can I talk about this with you later?"

"Yes, sweetheart, just tell me you love me and when you are coming home."

"Of course, I do. I love you with all my heart and I'll be home before you know it. We are almost at the end of this," I reassured her that I was okay as we said goodnight and ended our call. I walked back upstairs to my room, packed away the phone, and got ready to go to bed.

I took a drink of cold water and turned out the light. With the exception of a faint glow sneaking through from around the edges of the door, it was dark and quiet. I could hear the occasional Humvee as it drove away and the hum of distant generators running, but they mostly served as white noise. I lay down in bed, placed my small CD player on my chest, and put the earphones over my head. I pondered for a moment what Nadaleane had said. My wife was devoutly religious and was sure about what she believed. At that specific moment, I wasn't quite convinced. Maybe there was something in the dark that we did not see, something more plausible.

Most Christians believe that angels do not just exist, but that they come from heaven and walk the earth. The Bible has given us many examples of these spiritual beings that came to advise, forewarn, and help many biblical figures. However, they were winged beings dressed in white, not soldiers dressed in body armor carrying a machine gun. The angels described in the Bible were like what we see on TV, or maybe not. Could this angel have been what we needed at the time, a soldier?

If someone had asked me if I was a good person, I'd have said my early adult years were not the model for what many would consider Christian. I'd soften the brutal truth by saying I'm a work in progress. My behavior in my thirty-something years had been slightly better, but far from settled down. However, shortly after the birth of my son, something seemed to click as to how misplaced some of my priorities were. Even so, it still took a while to realign many of my old habits. I was not a serial killer or a preacher. I was acceptably in the middle of the two, and I had made some overall good decisions in my life in spite of myself. Nevertheless, we were human, and therefore prone to fall far short of what I believed a benevolent and just God required.

We had a chaplain with us in the battalion and church services were regularly held, but I was rarely able to attend, mostly due to either a work schedule or a mission schedule. I tried to compensate for my lack of worship attendance with almost nightly prayers. These usually centered around what I wanted or needed and not so much about giving thanks. It puzzled me as to why Nadaleane believed so earnestly that I had seen an angel. I was almost certain that there were other solders more deserving and certainly more accepting of a celestial encounter than Gerhard, Osborne, and me.

Osborne was Jewish. I knew his faith was dear to him, but we never actually talked about it very often and certainly never in any detail. We were not sure what Gerhard actually believed, but we were pretty sure, whatever it was, he had thrown it all to the wind the day he set foot in Iraq. The environment in Iraq actually skews a person's beliefs to the point that any one of us could look in the mirror and not recognize the person looking back. Even so, could I open my mind up to the possibility that something happened that could never be explained any other way? Many questions ran through my head, as I lay there almost ready to push the button on the CD player. What had we done to warrant this little nugget of gold? Was he a saint or a soldier? Who deserves or receives mercy, the people furthest from God or the people closest? The question I asked myself most was this: Were we passing through his life, or was he passing through our lives? The latter would indicate that our meeting was not coincidental, that it had to be us, and not just any three soldiers in Iraq. It meant that our success was important in the larger scheme of things. The answer would reveal more about faith and fate than I believe we could understand. I wasn't ready to take on the answer at that moment or at any time in the near future. I was not a theologian and didn't want to study the "what ifs" of the world or this war.

On any other day it probably would not have mattered, but on that day, we knew we were going home soon. Far too many movies had ended with the hero dying or getting blown up on his last mission. Internally, we were all understandably a little bit nervous, but by this time, we had already been in Iraq for a year or more. We had all been on extended missions, and, generally, all of us had seen our fair share of combat. During our tours, we had been mortared, rocketed, had truck bombs driven at us, come under small arms fire, fought riots, and treated the wounded or dying. We considered ourselves appropriately battle hardened. We were prepared and had done everything correctly, or as correctly as possible.

However, on this day, we couldn't have prevented that bus from stopping on that bridge. If it had been at a certain point earlier in our tours, we may not have known how to react nor had the presence of mind to respond as quickly. We were non-commissioned officers. We were sergeants, so our job was to solve problems. Nevertheless, on this night, we were dealt a hand of cards putting us in a highly disadvantaged position. If this mystery soldier had not shown up, would the overall outcome still have been the same? Maybe or maybe not. I doubt there would be any real way of knowing for sure. Will one of us stumble into a chance meeting with a soldier one day who hears this story and says he was the guy at the bridge that night? Maybe, I almost expect it.

For now, we are content that he was who my wife says he was, an angel sent to give us just a little help when we needed it and then step back into the shadows and watch to see if we made it count. In all truth, he was both a saint and a soldier.

I'm sleepy, and I don't want to think anymore today, I said to myself. My finger found the play button on the CD player lying on my chest. I pressed it until I heard a slight click and waited a few seconds for the music to start. I heard the low, soulful voice of Tom Jones gently singing "Green, Green Grass of Home." My mind began to relax and unravel from the day. I could feel my body giving in to the exhaustion. Somewhere between the twilight of barely awake and sleep, I mumbled a familiar, short prayer before I totally fell off. "*Lord, please forgive me of my sins.*

Lord, bless my parents, my wife, my son, and my fellow soldiers. Lord, please don't take me out of the fight, but just give me the strength, courage and wisdom to get through it. In Christ's name I pray, Amen." With those final words, I closed my eyes and drifted to sleep; knowing that whatever came with tomorrow would be here soon enough.

Who Are You?

On February 4, 2005, our plane touched down at McGuire Air Force Base, New Jersey, and we were shuttled to nearby Ft. Dix. There was snow on the ground, and it was cold. A General stood at the door of the plane to shake our hand as we exited. The company was assigned to a barracks building for our brief stay as we out-processed. I immediately found a room, threw my duffel bags on a bunk, and walked back outside to breathe in the cold, fresh American air. Standing just outside the door against the wall was another soldier who was like a brother to me, Staff Sergeant Anthony Sadler. "Big T," as I called him, was staring up at the blue sky and just taking a deep breath. I looked at Tony and said, "We made it; we made it home." Tony replied, "Yes, we did, Sgt. Wasserman. Yes, we did."

I asked Tony if I could borrow his cell phone for a few minutes to call my parents and my wife to let them know we had landed. He handed me his phone without saying a word. I dialed the number and heard the phone ring a few times before my mother finally picked up.

"Mom, it's me," I said.

"Gerit!" she exclaimed.

"Yes, Mom, it's me," I said again. "I'm not going to talk long. I'm tired, a little hungry, and need a shower, but I'm on American soil. I am good to go, mom."

I heard my mother say, "Thank God." There was a slight pause, and within a second or two, my mother started to cry. She handed the phone over to my dad. I had a brief conversation with him, said I would see them soon, and hurriedly went through the same routine with Nadaleane. I asked her not to come up for a day or two so we could get out-processed, but I knew that she was already on the road before I had even hung up. I handed the phone back to Tony, slapped him on the shoulder, and headed back into the building to take a shower and get some sleep. Our company spent the next week out-processing and getting used to the real world again. We enjoyed the luxuries of take-out Chinese food and hot pizza deliveries as we watched the Super Bowl on TV. Home was Home.

The next day did come soon enough and then came the next day, and then the next, and the one after that. Then one morning I woke up, and I was not staring at a concrete ceiling with a rusted metal hook cemented in it.

I sat up in bed, looked into a mirror and asked the person looking back, "Who are you? Where am I?"

I stood up, walked a few feet, and found I had a toilet, a sink, and a shower in the same room, mere steps away from my sleeping area, I mean, bedroom. I had a bedroom. I peed in the toilet and pressed a vaguely familiar small, silver lever that flushed it. I stood there for a second and watched clear water swirl away.

Taking a single side step, I was in front of a white sink counter and another mirror. Again, I asked the stranger that stared back, "Who are you?" Sighing, I looked at him again and asked, "What have you done?"

On the counter next to the sink, I found a new toothbrush and a new tube of toothpaste that was not in a dusty black shaving bag. I squeezed a white line of goo onto the brush and began to brush my teeth, still staring at the person in the mirror. I turned on the water, rinsed out my brush, sipped a handfull and spit it back into the sink. I let the water run for a few seconds and thought, *I can let it run all day, and it will never run out.* I shut off the spigot, walked back, and sat down on the bed. Again, I was looking into a mirror and staring at a stranger. I asked myself, "Where in the hell did all of these mirrors come from?"

I lay my head back on the pillow, stretched out an aching body. I could smell bacon cooking with banana pancakes and hot syrup. My wife was in the kitchen of our apartment fixing me breakfast. She had moved in after I deployed and had been there less than a year. I was vaguely familiar with the new abode and had not gotten used to my surroundings. I lay there, staring at the plaster swirl ceiling for a few minutes and thought that maybe I should put a metal hook in it. I was uncomfortable with being comfortable. The sheets were clean and smelled fresh; the apartment was warm; everything I needed was just steps away. I could hear the TV in the living room. At the time, life could not have been any better, but I wanted to go back to Iraq.

Where was my weapon? I felt naked without it. What if the building came under attack during the night? Didn't anyone understand what could happen?

I sat back up and began to pull drawers open looking for my uniform, I mean clothes. I now had clothes. They were all different, with different colors. "*Find something brown*," I said to myself. I discovered a pair of jeans and a brown shirt, got dressed, and walked into a little kitchen to enjoy breakfast with my wife. I grabbed a plate that was sitting on the counter and walked by the stove looking for the food, when my wife asked me, "What are you doing?"

What am I doing? Chow line? "Never mind," I said and sat down to a home-cooked breakfast prepared by the loving hands of my wife, thinking, *I'm not sure I can live like this—I want to go back.*

I hadn't finished the job. There were still things that needed to be done and we needed, I mean, *they* needed experienced soldiers to get the mission completed. Besides, I was a stranger here, a foreigner in a foreign home. I was no good here. I needed to get back to my unit. How did I get here anyway? Where were my medical bag and my weapons, and why were there so many damn mirrors in this building? I mean, apartment. My wife was not just a voice at the other end of the phone anymore. She was real.

"Are you done, sweetie pie?" my wife asked. "You said you wanted to go see your sister and visit your mom and dad again, right?"

"Yes, yes, I'm finished dear. It was good, thank you. Just let me get my socks and boots, I mean, shoes on, and I'll be ready to go."

We walked downstairs through a small breezeway toward my wife's car. She handed me the keys, refreshed that she did not have to drive for the first time in a long time. She finally felt that she had her husband back and we could pick up life right where we had left off. We got in the car, and it felt comfortable. I enjoyed the experience of driving a normal car around town instead of the bulky military vehicles. We pulled through the parking lot, made a right turn, and drove past the gas stations, the restaurants, the mall, and Home Depot. *Wow*, I thought, *all of this in one place, too easy.*

My wife grabbed my arm and slid her hand down into mine. My fingers wrapped around hers as we drove past the shopping centers and restaurants. I exited onto the interstate and headed to my sister's house, thirty minutes away. I took a deep breath and exhaled the tension. I relaxed. Being home was good. Remembering the route back to my sister's house had challenges, I believed there were two overpasses that I would have to negotiate, I mean, drive under.

Easy peasy, I thought, as we drove down the highway. I stayed in the right lane until I got used to the regular traffic pattern again as we drove through the first overpass. I changed lanes unexpectedly and heard a horn blowing over my shoulder. I looked into the rear view mirror, the one mirror I seemed to respect, and scanned the overpass for combatants, I mean, people. My wife clamped down on my hand, slightly alarmed, and asked, "What are you doing, Gerit?"

What am I doing? I just cut someone off on the highway trying to changes lanes. "Didn't you see that squirrel that started to run onto the highway, sweetie-pie?" I asked. *Good recovery,* I thought. I couldn't tell her that there could have been someone with an RPG on the overpass. It would scare her too much. It was best to keep those things to myself, maybe tell just the people I could trust. *My buddies, they know. They understand how dangerous it is out here, I mean, out there. I'm home now. It isn't necessary to worry about those sorts of things.*

It was the weekend. We'd have a nice lunch, maybe a glass of wine, or go do a little shopping. I would go to church on Sunday, and everyone would be back to work on Monday morning. No one seemed to notice the apparent sound of an explosion that just went off down the road, I mean the trash truck that was empting the dumpster at Burger King. It sure sounded like an explosion. *How can everyone act like we're not fighting for our lives? Don't they remember we're in a war? I don't know if I can do this—I need to go back.*

My sister was glad to see me and ran out to give me a big hug as we pulled into the driveway. Her house was neat as a pin, and, as always, she had something interesting and wonderful on the stove. We would be treated to a great lunch.

"Have you seen Mom and Dad yet?" my sister asked.

"Of course," I said, "I caught them yesterday as I was coming in. I didn't stay long; I just wanted to get home, but I'm heading there again as soon as I leave here."

"What about Kyle?" she asked.

"Not yet, he doesn't even know I'm home," I told her. "I've talked with his mom, and I'm planning on showing up at school on Monday to surprise him."

'Well," my sister said with a sheepish look and hesitated, "I want to throw you a little welcome home party, but give me a little time to pull it together. I'll need you to give me a list of people to invite. Mom, Nadaleane, and I will plan it."

"Great, it sounds like fun" I said. "I'll start working on a list tonight and get it to ya."

Her husband, Gary, and I migrated to the living room, and I settled my body down on her extremely comfortable leather sofa. My sister handed me a glass of wine and twelve months of tension just seemed to seep out of me. I almost felt guilty for being this relaxed. We talked, and the conversation with normal people was enjoyable. No acronyms to decipher. Sentences were long and coherent, not the two word responses that my language had been reduced to, such as: Move out, how copy, yes sir, roger that, incoming, or he's dead. Finally, normal words from normal people. Maybe I just needed a little time to adjust.

"So, how was it over there, Gerit?" my brother-in-law asked. I hesitated to answer. He seemed interested in my perspective of my tour, but what did he truly want to know? How was it for me, or for everyone else? Did he want to know about the attacks, the wounded men, the firefights, the lies I had told Mom and Dad, the people killed, the heat, the smell, and the sounds ringing in my ears? What type of answer did he want? Why didn't he ask me if the wine was good or how it felt to put on a pair of jeans again? I felt the real meaning of his question was obvious. He wanted me to say we were failing or we had made a mistake. Maybe I was reading too much into his question. Nadaleane didn't especially want to hear any of the war stories or the blood and guts recollections. It made her cringe, and she just wanted to talk about anything but Iraq. Nadaleane wanted some sign of normalcy again. Why would anyone ask me this question?

"Oh, it was a hoot Gary. Very interesting," I said. I played it off as if my tour was no big deal. Like a lot of things, people ask questions as if they want to know the answers, but in reality they don't want to know. It gets boring or it has more information than they really wanted to hear or maybe I wasn't ready to answer.

We had a spectacular lunch of some of my sister's home cooked recipes and a good wine, not too dry. She had fixed a pot roast cooked with spices, garlic potatoes slow cooked on the grill, and fresh salad picked from her garden. We spent the late morning to early afternoon hours talking lightly about coming home and getting back to the proverbial normal. But what was normal? I wasn't so sure anymore. Every once in a while I could feel that a darker personality tried to peek from behind the white curtain of a ripple-less pond. Had someone moved what I believed was normal?

I hugged my sister, said good-bye, and thanked her for inviting me over and all that she had done for me while I was gone. My wife and I got back into the car and then drove to my parents' house. It was almost a repeat of the warm family welcome, but no dinner this time around. If I weren't careful, I'd be eating myself into a new wardrobe. My mom was ecstatic to see me and gave me a big hug. She wanted to hear everything. I mean, she thought she wanted to hear everything. Mostly, she just wanted to recount the phone call I made home when I got to Ft. Dix. Mom also showed me a calendar that she wrote on every day while I was overseas. She wrote down every time that I called and everything about the war that she saw on the news.

The calendar was practically a diary and it was literally full with events.

My dad, a former Marine, had a better idea of what I had experienced and probably knew I wasn't ready to discuss everything right away. Our conversations were more about the gang at Hardees or my rental property, the practical stuff. We would eventually deal with the business issues, but for now, I enjoyed not having the responsibility of taking care of everything that everyone else had been doing for me. I was a far cry from being quiet, but I was mostly asking questions of everyone else. What had I missed? What had changed? We talked about almost everything but Iraq and I certainly didn't bring up anything about seeing angels or ghosts on the battlefield. I didn't want people to think that I had gone crazy.

I had essentially lived life in a plastic bubble while the rest of the world kept moving. I needed to catch up. In the short period I had been home, I had already noticed that the price of gas had gone up nearly a buck, milk and bread cost more and I had bills that came in the mail and via e-mail that I now needed to handle myself. I had forgotten what my daily life required.

We visited with mom and dad for a respectable amount of time, nearly three hours and I was finding it hard to relax with the idea of being home. It was good to have parents and family, but before I knew it, I felt tired, almost exhausted. The emotional reconnections, the jetlag, and time change had messed up my sleep pattern. I was falling hard and fast. I had to say good-bye and hugged my mom and dad while letting them know I would come over again tomorrow. I could see that mom especially felt relief that her son was home.

In a few minutes, I would be back in the apartment, kicking off my shoes and resting. Maybe I would take a nap or go straight to bed for the evening. I could do either; I was on my time now.

I had a few weeks before I had planned to return to work, and I didn't need to wake up at any certain time. I lay my head on the pillow and stared at an empty white ceiling.

In the coming days, weeks, and months my adjustment back into the world I had left wasn't as easy as it had been to leave. Eager to serve my country, I had packed my bags and had gone to war nearly fourteen months ago. For the people that I left behind, it created a black hole of emotion in their lives. The void was created because they loved me and were concerned about what was happening to me. They felt my pain, understood my fears, and enjoyed my triumphs, but they couldn't share with me their fears or their problems. They had allowed me to focus on the mission, in essence, to focus on me. I could not have left them behind any more than they could forget I was gone, but distance, time, and circumstances took a toll on the relationships.

While I was deployed nearly worry free, my family had taken up everything else that I would normally contend with during a typical day or a week. This was good for me, but it added stress to my family members, who already had aching hearts. I am sure I had taken this for granted, and I almost certainly did not recognize the added strain on the relationships. As a matter of fact, within six months of returning home, most of the important affiliations were either damaged or in serious trouble.

My return to work did not go as well as I had hoped, either. My wife and I would sometimes fall into arguments at the blink of an eye, and overall, I seemed to be angry at the casual nature in which we, as a nation, conducted ourselves while engaged in two major conflicts. Overseas, men and women were dying, and for what? So that we could go to the *Outback Steakhouse* on Friday night or hit the clubs on Saturday night and go to church on Sunday to ask for forgiveness for Saturday, before going back to work on Monday? The average person in the U.S. barely noticed the two wars. In a military town, they attracted a little more attention, but for the most part, it was not in the headlines anymore. We were four years past 9/11, and it appeared that we were getting war weary, and I was mad about it. People didn't seem to care, and nothing seemed to be going that well for me.

I sought solace in church, but carried my misgivings in with me and sat mostly in the rear of the Sunday school class or in the rear of the auditorium. I rarely spoke to anyone, and when I did, I kept it brief. Sitting in the back, I was able to leave almost as soon as the closing hymns started, avoiding people who might have talked to me if they had caught me. I was being called the angry guy at the back of the church. I didn't care. I *was* the angry guy at the back of the church. I was mad at the people in the church and the whole group of hypocrites who occupied the pews next to me every week.

I called them the twice a year patriots. They waved the flag on the Fourth of July and Memorial Day, and maybe on Veteran's Day, but the rest of the year, they just headed out to dinner on Friday night, sinned on Saturday, and went back to church on Sunday. This added more fuel to an already smoldering fire. Things were not getting better overseas, and the further our nation moved past 9/11, the less we seemed to care about the military, much less the deployed soldiers who were dying on the battlefield. The history of the world is about conflict and I didn't understand how everyone seemed to miss the one we were in.

One morning after Sunday school, someone asked why I continued to come to that church if it was that miserable. "Find another church," they said. I had asked myself the same question. It was obvious to me that it didn't make a difference one way or the other. I had prayed for God to forgive me of my sins, which were different from other people's sins. Yet nothing in my life seemed to be any better or any worse. I thought that these were the very people who pounded the war drums years before, but now had all but forgotten the noise they made as thousands of men and women were loaded on airplanes and mailed off to defend our nation. Some were mailed back in metal containers, and the rest stepped back onto ambivalent soil. Encouragement from people within the congregation usually came in the form of a quoted Bible verse or two, as if they had done their duty. Or they had nothing at all to say. I honestly tried to talk with a few people who I had felt might understand, but everyone seemed to lack the ability to personally interact or have any empathy for the experience.

Eight months or more after I had returned home, I sat in my sister's living room one afternoon almost in tears with disgust as I lamented on my misgivings. I shared the story of the man on the bridge after Nadaleane had leaked it to her. I gave her the details and watched as she sat with her mouth gapped open listening as I told her in a matter of fact tone. "Gerit, you need to write this down," she said. "What a story you have." I wasn't ready to do that and said as much as I continued to express my disappointment in the coming weeks. The event was never far from my mind, but the further I moved away from the date, the less it seemed to mean, and I attached no special significance to it and had temporarily forgotten how unusual it had been when it happened.

The meager recognitions given to our servicemen and women during two or three holidays a year were not enough for what I believe our fighting men and women were giving to the remaining 99% of the population. America sat home, flipped through 200 channels of fantasy, and lost connection to a soldier's reality. The religious barely gave those special days a glancing blow. They all but threw a wreath on a grave and rushed off to *Golden Corral* for that free dinner. My frustration grew and I continued to struggle with the question. No immediate answer surfaced that gave me the reason I would continue with anything that wasn't giving me the payoff that I wanted. Neither job, marriage, church; the solid foundations of my life did not seem to be holding together quite so solid. I had believed that if you stuck with anything, sooner or later, it would have an influence on you, either good or bad. This time around, however, all effort was falling flat on all fronts.

The January date that was planned as a reunion grew closer, and the events of that night re-haunted my thoughts again. My sister had told my mom, who now wanted to hear the story herself, about the "angel" on the bridge. Still I wasn't sure, and I had no answer as to the "who" or "why" of that night. What could it have been? What was it I needed to hear myself say?

The answer, as it turned out, was right in front to my eyes, hidden in plain sight. In the pages of the Bible and in the duties of my life, an answer emerged. A light bulb came on that made me believe that my service, my sacrifice, and who I had become was worth it and maybe I just needed time to figure it out. The layers of the why began to peel themselves back, and at the core was the reason any of us would be willing to go all in for the ones we loved. The "guy" at the bridge was just the example of what Gerhard, Oz, and I had been doing all along for each other; going the extra mile. And there was the answer. Selfless Service wasn't for us after all; it was for everyone else. Nothing said it had to be appreciated, but it had to be given. I was sure that I hadn't invented this concept, but if I believed this way, so did many others. That belief has been manifested in many good charitable organizations and veteran groups that go the well-known extra mile.

The main reason I continued to attend church where I did was because it was the only place that my son had ever gone. He had grown up in that church with many of the kids his age. I was doing it for him. It was one small act of unselfishness. He didn't make it every Sunday, but on the weekends he was with me, we went together. I saw no reason to yank him away from what I believed to be a stable situation. I thought, *I'm not exactly happy, but he is, so why upset the apple cart?*

I searched deeper and found men better than I, who had given more than I had, with little or no accolades. Suddenly, my little gripes seemed almost minute in comparison and not worth the time I had given them. The firemen that scaled the stairs in the World Trade Center on 9/11 undoubtedly never considered that morning at breakfast that they would not be having dinner with their families. It wasn't intended to turn out that way, but for the love of their fellow man, they chose a profession that would ultimately hand them their deaths.

Although many jobs are hazardous, most people don't go to work believing that they won't come home at the end of the day. And yet, the soldiers, sailors, marines and airmen did that every day they were deployed down range, in combat. It is a job where someone can legally order someone else, or be ordered, to his or her death. If the captain said to take that hill, well, we took that hill. It might be costly in terms of lives, but that was what the job required. The recognition of a payment in blood was what made the difference between great leaders and so-so leaders. In history, there were men who wasted lives, and men who valued lives. History has judged them.

Peeling back another layer, I found several passages in the Bible where Christ himself acknowledged the tough job of being a soldier and offered redemption to the warrior. Why was this not discussed at church? We were in a war. In the eighth chapter of Matthew, Jesus healed the centurion's servant based on his faith, and his faith amazed Jesus. In all, there are seven soldiers or centurions in the New Testament, and all are looked upon favorably. Roman soldiers nailed Jesus to the cross, and he asked for forgiveness for them because they did not know what they were doing. It was a centurion, a soldier that gave the final accounts of Christ's death as he hung on the cross. The account of the centurion at the cross is mentioned in all four of the gospels, and it provides what I believe is a final salute to the weary warrior.

For all of the pomp, circumstance, and ceremony typically associated with the military, it is still the dirty business of man killing his fellow man. I believe that Jesus knew the unpleasant job was necessary to accomplish God's overall plan, and maybe he held a special place in his heart for soldiers. What did soldiers have that others didn't? Greater faith, so it seemed. They had to have it. Few other selected professions see the absolute worst that man has to offer and still believe that there has to be a greater hope than all of the evil that can exist. Maybe I just needed to find this out on my own, and in my own painful manner. And maybe that "soldier" at the bridge was just there to make sure that we made it across, figuratively speaking.

If that were the case, then there was a redemption and hope for me, and that hope didn't depend on anyone else. All it required was for me to accept it and have the faith of the centurion. Make it count, and live up to the blood payment made 2,000 years ago and yesterday.

The Cost of Angels—Epilogue

ON FEBRUARY 10, 2005, HEADQUARTERS Company of the 391st MP Battalion said their goodbyes and departed Ft. Dix, New Jersey for their homes and families. The bulk of the company boarded busses and headed to Ohio. Some of us who were cross-leveled into the company got on a plane or a bus or had someone pick us up. Other companies that had made up the battalion came in, went through the same process, and eventually left Ft. Dix for their families as well.

Approximately a month later, I was released from active duty and received orders assigning me back to the 80th Division. I was allowed three months off from attending drills while I integrated back into the stateside world. During the time after I was released from active duty, I had reported in by telephone, but the official orders eventually came in from the Department of the Army assigning me back to my home unit and I would have to attend drill again the following month. At the time, the 80th was forming its own battle roster for a rotation into Iraq, and amazingly enough, my name showed up on the list. A platoon sergeant started leaving me messages and sending me e-mails. At first I just ignored them, believing that they must have been sent by mistake. However, it was not a mistake. They had me down for the next rotation that was going over.

After just coming home three months before, I knew I could get released from these orders. But did I actually want to be released? I believed that I could do one more rotation easily. A big part of something inside my gut genuinely wanted to go. I ran the idea by my wife and parents. Needless to say, the idea did not go over well.

In July 2005, I reported to the unit after returning from overseas and received what I would call a somewhat tepid reception. The excitement and support that I had early in the deployment had died down. A new leadership that did not know me had transitioned in and immediately began pressuring me to make a decision to reenter the drill sergeants' academy program. They wanted me to get through it and be ready to be deployed again. As a matter of fact, the few folks who remembered me and were still around were my platoon leader, Lt. Sharpe and the operations sergeant. Lt. Sharpe had done a great job helping my wife and keeping in touch with me while I was gone, while single-handedly running the family support group for the unit. Towards the end of it all I think she was getting a little burned out and felt underappreciated. Overall Lt. Sharpe was the unsung hero of this story.

I went home after that weekend and did not tell my wife anything about the conversation that had taken place during the drill. When I looked into her eyes, I could see hurt from those months I had been gone. So much of the worst of what I was living over there and did not explain was on the nightly news and in the headlines of the local papers. My son had missed me and often asked when I was coming home. In his eight-year-old mind, whenever someone asked about me while I was gone, he had boiled it down to this reality: that his daddy was in Iraq fighting the bad guys. The deployment had added a stress to my parents' lives as well. My dad, who had always covered my gaps, told me that the next time I left I was taking my wife and my mom with me. They had been watching the nightly news too much, and that, coupled with my location, kept their nerves on edge, whether they expressed it or not.

The decision should have been easy, but it was emotionally very difficult for me to make. I loved the Army and believed in the values it represented.

In August of 2005, I left the military behind and transitioned into the retired reserves. In essence, I retired. My company commander asked me several times if this was what I genuinely wanted to do. I hesitated and stumbled over the decision each time he would ask me throughout the day, but I always came back to the main reason I considered retiring, my family. On Sunday afternoon, after the drill weekend was over, the unit bought a cake and gave me a small gift to say goodbye. I drove home with the sun in my eyes trying to console myself that I had made the right decision. I knew that I had, but I also felt a sense of emptiness, and a big question loomed. *What now?*

Several months passed when I sat down one evening and put pen to paper, trying to define the "what now" question. I had a lot going on and a lot on my mind. I made a list of everything I felt I wanted or needed to accomplish in my life. I had come home from Iraq feeling a sense of purpose and a compulsion to get something done. I wasn't sure how long these feelings were going to last, and I needed to capitalize on them while I had them. Completing this book was barely on that list. I had given over twenty years of service with a mixture of active duty, National Guard time, and reserve time to my country. Now that all of my service was in the rearview mirror, I needed to ask myself what it all meant and if it counted for anything. My answer was almost instant, but I needed to hear myself say it in order to believe it. Yes, it did. It was valuable, and I have no regrets.

I was lucky enough to go into the Army with a good friend I had grown up with, Rodney Quick, and after basic training and advanced individual training, we were placed into the same platoon in the same National Guard unit. That unit and the soldiers who were in it at the time taught me a great deal about friendships, looking out for the man next to you, training, doing your job, completing the mission, and, most of all, leadership. After our unit was reorganized ten years into my career, many of us tried to stay together as we sought new positions in the National Guard. However, it wasn't long before we had been scattered to the four winds, and I had started what became the second half of my career. During the first half, I was more or less the follower, but the second half provided me with opportunities to be more of a leader. By this time, I had obtained my associate's degree, was striving for more education, and had established a solid civilian career within the architectural-engineering and construction field.

The Army had received a lot of bad press from the Abu Ghraib scandal, and our unit was tarred with the same brush as those who were actually involved with the abuse itself. Although we were not there at that time, the media story broke after we got there. In the public's mind, it might as well have been us. In reality, we were in the process of cleaning up that mess and correcting all of the mistakes that had been made. I saw nothing like what was described in the media and saw Army values held to the highest degree.

It is difficult to say which quality or value has the most importance. All are important and necessary. However, to me, along with those values, training and leadership also stand out as essential for any mission or any task to be successful. I believed that the abuse scandal resulted from that very breakdown of training and mindful leadership. It was not for me to judge, but I, like everyone else, had an opinion. From my early days in the National Guard until I retired, I was fortunate to have been assigned with units that always had good leaders and set good examples. Every unit will have its share of new, inexperienced personnel, and every unit will have a job to perform. Their success depends on how well they can work together, which depends on how well they train and how well they are led, but sometimes, just sometimes, it may depend on more.

On January 12, 2005, three soldiers stepped onto a dark road in Iraq. Maybe their destiny wasn't written. Maybe the outcome had not yet been determined. Maybe the forces of evil and the forces of good crossed swords in an unseen battle, and the victor would step over the fallen foe, and emerge from the shadows to direct or redirect the destinies of three soldiers, who were in charge of forty-two prisoners, and those of many other soldiers involved in a much larger battle. In the grand scheme of things, all of those destinies would intertwine with other destinies to shape a larger, defined future. What was our role in this plan? What was our destiny? Were we supposed to die in a firefight on the side of that road that night? No, we weren't. A soldier emerged into the lights, with the ink still wet on our providence, and he simply asked, "Do you fellows need a hand?" Perhaps with those few words, he wrote a future that we had not yet lived and we would never truly understand, a future based on what we did with the gift. I knew I couldn't change the world or change the mind of everyone I met. I couldn't solve every problem that crossed my path or even offer a good suggestion most of the time. What I could change was me, and I would try. There, I left my faith and my hope. All that mattered that night was that He was there.

Honoring our promise not to forget that day or forget the friends that we lost, on January 12, 2006, Osborne and I met in Gatlinburg, Tennessee. Gerhard, who was in New Orleans, Louisiana, helping with the Hurricane Katrina cleanup, phoned in his attendance. The three of us, and sometimes others, still meet on January 12th, every year.

I returned from Iraq with an enhanced belief that life has to be lived at the ground level, running, not just watched as a spectator while sitting in the "cheap seats." What I mean is that you have to be involved, doing the best you can do, doing what you profess and doing what you know how to do. It also means learning and getting your boots muddy if that's what it takes. I owe much to the men and women I have served with in various capacities over the years. They have helped me get my boots muddy. They have given me friendships, opportunities and encouragement that have allowed me to become a better person and a better soldier and to accomplish my life's tasks at that ground level perspective. Before I deployed to Iraq, I may have thought of myself as average, but I am average among the less than 1% of the finest men and women who put on the uniform and defend this nation every day. Because of them, and alongside them, I am above average. They lift me up and inspire me to be a better person.

Before my tour would end, two people would be killed whom I had a personal connection with in Iraq and three more would die over the next two years after I got home. If you had asked any one of them if the sacrifice was worth it, I believe that all would say, yes. If you were to ask the families of these fallen heroes' the same question, I imagine that you would get mixed reactions, but all of them would want their loved ones back home. They would question whether or not the price paid has held its value and if the nation had appreciated the sacrifice. They will want to know if the lonely nights, missed birthdays and pointless holidays have gained us any more freedom or made us any safer as a nation.

I believe that all of the families of service members who were lost believe that their angel was taken from them prematurely and would trade golden wings for a pair of kicked off shoes at the back door. Grief alone cannot express what the families have gone through over the years and what they will be asked to endure as life marches on. In some cases a wife may feel guilty for being able to move on with her life and forgetting the subtle nuances that made her husband special. A teenage daughter cries over forgetting the sound of her daddy's voice or forgetting his scent on his clothing when he would give her a hug. Forgetting may help ease the pain, but it will never erase the feelings of why we love them. I have dedicated this last chapter to the memory of those who I knew, and will miss with all my heart. I hope that I never forget them, but just in case my memory begins to fade, I hope these few words will remind me how wonderful they were on earth as they are in heaven.

On November 2, 2004 ECP East came under intense small arms fire from a village across the main highway that ran outside the prison. Sgt. Hinkle, one of my fellow soldiers from first squad and Sgt. Horton who had been with me in Ganci 3 were both pinned down and shooting it out with the attacking insurgents. The perimeter towers engaged with .50 caliber machine guns, but the distance and concealment reduced their effectiveness and the battle continued for almost an hour. Bullets were coming in over the wall and ricocheted around inside the FOB as they struck concrete barriers and masonry buildings.

Gerhard, Osborne and I were maintaining our position at Level I Alpha and were just generally trying to stay out of the way of all of the lead that was flying around. At some point a detainee in the camp was struck in the leg with a ricocheting bullet and collapsed to the ground in the open. The bullet had entered the man's calf and exited through his shin, shattering his tibia. Nearby detainees dragged the man as close as possible to the entrance gate of the camp, but retreated as the battle outside the wall intensified. Sgt. Dan Fannin and I grabbed the keys to the cage, went inside and drug the wounded detainee out and onto a stretcher behind a protective barrier, but the ten yards or so between us and the CP was exposed to intense small arms fire. Oz shuttled medical supplies and Sgt. Fannin inserted an IV in the man's arm. I had opened two large field dressings and was wrapping the detainee's leg as he was screaming in pain.

On the other side of the FOB a civilian contracting company had an area set up to support their employees and their mission. They had a section designated for sleeping and shower trailers similar to our arrangement. The contracting company also had several trailers they used specifically for offices and others were for storage. A contract employee, Jeff Serrett, was a fire fighter and an Emergency Medical Technical or EMT that was brought in to help establish a fire department presence similar to that of military posts back in the states. He was the civilian version of the army medic and we respectfully called him "Doc." Jeff was a big man and was a frequent face around the FOB, specifically at the field hospital. I had run into him numerous times at the chow hall or around the MWR area and knew him well enough to say hello or make casual conversation. Gearheart had the most interaction with him because of their presence together at the hospital and he was easy to spot. He usually wore a big straw cowboy hat and had a very likeable manner about him.

At approximately the same time frame that Sgt. Fannin and I were dealing with the wounded detainee, Jeff Serrett opened the door to his office while the battle was still under way and was struck by a ricocheting round in his lower stomach area, which traveled through into his leg and hit an artery. Some people have said that they thought he heard what sounded like a knock on the door, opened it and caught the next round. It is hard to conceive that anyone could have heard the firefight taking place and mistake the bullets striking on the side of the trailer for someone knocking on a door. Jeff tried to instruct the people helping what they should do before passing out from the loss of blood. His coworkers and fellow soldiers slid him onto a metal door and drove him to the field hospital as quickly as they could.

Simultaneously, I had jumped in with the detainee in the ambulance heading to the same field hospital. As soon as he was turned over I would catch a ride back to the camp. The driver wheeled the ambulance into a courtyard-like area just outside the emergency room and backed as close as he could to a set of double doors. I jumped from the back and yelled for medics that were standing just inside the door. Together we unloaded the detainee, put him on a stretcher, and pushed him into the emergency room. In a flurry of activity we wheeled him up next to an exam table and everyone lifted together to transfer him onto the table, pushing the gurney aside. I had noticed another man on the other table, but hadn't paid much attention to exactly who it was. Now that the urgency was over I stood back and took a deep breath and saw a familiar face. It was Doc!

He appeared unconscious, pale and his clothes had been cut away. A team of nurses and doctors were crowded around him, taking his vital signs and obviously trying to save his life.

I asked a nurse, "What happened to Doc?"

"He was shot," she replied, "in the stomach, I think." I stood there for a minute and watched in disbelief. I didn't know Jeff extremely well, but I knew him. Unaware of it at the time, I was perhaps one of the last people to see him alive. I heard later that he had been evacuated to Germany and had died en route.

Our operations sections had called in Apache Gunships to aggressively suppress the small arms fire that pinned the soldiers down at ECP East. 'Aggressively suppress' is just army talk for shooting the hell out of the place until they stopped shooting back. I walked outside of the ER and leaned against the wall for a second. The firefight that had been taking place had ended. I thought about whom I had brought in and whom I had seen before I walked out . . . *not a fair trade,* I thought to myself. This seemingly small event would circle back around in my life in the coming years and having that fraction of information about a person's death, in the totality of his life is haunting. I have considered it a mixed blessing and the overall impact has been positive, but it too has had its cost.

On December 4, 2004 Cari Anne Gasiewicz was killed when an IED exploded as she made her way home from Abu Ghraib. Annie, as I knew her, was a linguist fluent in Arabic and assigned to an intelligence brigade working out of Abu. She worked more closely with our operations and intelligence sections, but occasionally made her way out to the camps. She would frequently disguise herself as an MP to gain intelligence information from the general conversations of the detainees.

We often had visitors come through the camps with international relief originations checking on the prisoners. There was usually a lot of talk between the relief workers and the detainees and we were never truly sure what they were saying. Annie would put on an MP bizarre, strap on a pistol, and stand out on the wire like one of us non-Arabic speaking MPs. The whole time she was taking in what they were saying and regularly going back into the CP tent writing up notes. The last time I remember this happening I was heading up to the chow hall to grab lunch for the rest of the guys working Ganci 3. I asked Annie if she wanted anything and she said to grab her a couple of hotdogs and some fries. In between running in and out writing her notes, she would try to grab a bite to eat.

Two months later Oz and Gerhard and I were sitting down in the chow hall for lunch when Spc. Gillman walked up and sat down with us.

"Hey, did you guys hear what happened to Gasiewicz?' Gillman asked.

"No, what?" I said, not expecting the most severe answer.

"She was killed the other day, on her way home," Gillman said in an almost unemotional manner and seemingly removed from the event. However nonchalantly he said it, I know he wasn't without some hurt. Gillman had worked alongside her more than we had, and I know that he felt the loss whether he showed it or not.

Osborne gasped, "What, you have got to be kidding me?

"Nope, not kidding," Gillman replied, "She was heading out, going to Kuwait for home and got hit with an IED." I put my food down and just stared at him for a minute and asked, "Is this for real Gillman? We just saw her. I guess it was a few weeks ago. Really Gillman?"

"Yeah Wass, sorry but it's true. I had just seen her a few days before myself in the operations section," Gillman said.

Almost instantly I felt my eyes well up and I couldn't say a word. I was stunned and speechless. I took a bite of food, chewed it slowly and briefly listened as the others discussed their own level of shock. In seconds our little lunch group fell silent. No one knew what to say and no one really wanted to talk. We quietly sat at the table, nibbled at our lunches, got up and left to go back to work. The unexpectedness of the news hit us like a bolt of lightning. Gasiewicz had been a good soldier. It could have been anyone of us who'd been killed. I started to feel I that I was leaving unfinished business or unsaid appreciation on the table. Emotionally we were caught off guard, but we did not have the luxury to dwell on the event and had to continue with our job. The unit would set up a small makeshift memorial, and we would pay our respects in our own way.

On May 5, 2006, Sgt. Nathan Vacho, the son of our Command Sergeant Major John Vacho, was killed when an IED exploded near his vehicle during combat operations in Baghdad, Iraq. Most of us in the unit did not know Nathan personally and he was not in Iraq during our deployment. However, since he was Sergeant Major Vacho's son, the news of his death was both personal and important to us and equally as shocking. A little more than a year after CSM Vacho had returned from a yearlong deployment, his son deployed to Iraq. On one of his first missions and within weeks of his arrival, Nathan was killed. He was all of us in some small way. He was every red blooded American young man wrapped up into one and I identified with him. He was on the high school football team, involved with numerous student activities and a member of the civil air patrol; something that I also enjoyed a kid. Nathan joined the Army reserve early in his life, earned his EMT certificate and later on, a Licensed Practical Nurse or LPN.

CSM Vacho spoke often of his family back in Wisconsin; he was proud of his heritage and the service that his family had given to this nation. Every night CSM Vacho would write a little something in his diary that he would eventually leave behind for his family and I am sure he made notes to his son. Sometimes, on his nightly strolls through the camps he would sit and read some of his thoughts to us from his diary. In a strange way, I felt that I knew Nathan through the words and actions of his father. If they were anything alike, then he was the finest of young men. In the years to come Oz and I would travel to a small Wisconsin town to help CSM Vacho and the rest of his family celebrate his son's life with a fundraiser that is held each year for local charities.

On June 1, 2007, Sgt. Bruce Horner was killed by sniper fire during a cordon and search mission in Seddah, Iraq. I got home from work that afternoon, ate dinner with my wife, and relaxed in our small apartment for the remainder of the day. Just before going to bed I decided to turn on the TV and watch the evening news. The lead story was about Bruce's death. I felt like my chest had just been hit with a hammer. I knew Bruce pretty well, and we had served together a few years earlier in another Military Police unit and we had deployed together to Germany in 1999 for operation Joint Guardian. After we returned in the spring of 2000, we went our separate ways and eventually Bruce returned to full time active duty. The last time I saw him was shortly after 9/11, while he was working the gate at a local military post. After passing through the tightened security I pulled over to the side of the road and Bruce and I took a few minutes to catch up on the latest news with each other.

Bruce was also a great Christian. He was heavily involved with his church and enjoyed helping in the teen department. He was the one person I knew who could balance the duality of being a soldier and solid Christian at the same time. I have asked myself a hundred times, why Bruce? His wife, Erin was nothing less than a pillar of strength, which I believe was derived from her faith. I went to the viewing and could barely hold it together as I walked past my friend. When I got to Erin she was completely magnanimous in her nature, and holding my hand, as she reassured me that Bruce loved God so much that he probably danced through the gates of heaven. You have to know him to believe it, but that was completely true.

On June 14, 2007 Sgt. Richard Parker was killed when his vehicle was struck with in IED in Iraq. Richard was a member of the Maine National Guard unit that was assigned to the 391st MP Battalion with us at Abu Ghraib in 2004, but he was not deployed with his Maine unit at the time of his death. He saw an opportunity to serve again and had volunteered for another tour after returning home. Of all of the units in the battalion, I had always felt that the Maine National Guard unit had the best Family Readiness Group (FRG), which indicated a real closeness among its members. Most of the members came from small surrounding towns such as Salem Township. The soldiers worked together in some manner in their civilian jobs and the families knew each outside of the military. When the news of Richard's death reached me through an e-mail, I couldn't immediately put a face with the name, but when I opened an attachment that had a photo of him, I immediately knew who he was and remembered him.

When the cost was totaled, 4403 soldiers, sailors, airmen and Marines would eventually give their lives in Iraq. Of that total number, 4398 I knew nothing about. However, five people had touched my life in different ways and to a different degree. Each of them left a family behind that wept for their loss and would try to recover from the pain. Silently, in their hearts they wondered why their sons or daughters or husbands or brothers or sisters were asked to sacrifice their lives. I can provide no good answer to the question and can offer a minimum amount of comfort that our Nation as a whole will always value the lives of its fallen warriors as long as there are veterans. We will continue to honor those who have given their all.

Acknowledgments

It took a long time to get this book in print. The majority of delays rest squarely on my shoulders, as I struggled with the right way to tell this story and wrestle with some of the feelings associated with it all along the way. However, different people encouraged me at different points in the process and deserve the recognition for playing a small part in the overall success of getting this book published. To my sister Terri who first suggested that I write the story down. To Osborne's mom, Sherry, who never doubted I would get it completed and told me how to make it look like a book. To Cheryl, who was the first to read the entire manuscript and was able to offer some valuable copy editing advice. To the Mcbean's that Oz and I met in Cozumel and encouraged me to get past a hump and finish the story; it was important. To Julia Dye who gave me a realistic perspective of what I was up against with regards to the publishing environment; this is what you'll face. To mom and dad who have believed in me since the day I was born and have encouraged me from that day forward. To my wife who was a big part of the story. To my son, who thinks it is just "cool." Last but not least I'd like to say thank you to Terry Trueman who helped me "get the ball over the goal line." We argued vigorously, debated the content and disagreed politically. Thank God we became friends. To everyone above and many, many more not mentioned . . . Thank You!